Our World, God's World

Reflections, readings and
prayers on the environment

The Bible Reading Fellowship
BRF encourages regular, informed Bible reading as a means of renewal in churches.
BRF publishes three series of regular Bible Reading Notes: *New Daylight*, *Guidelines* and *First Light*.
BRF publishes a wide range of materials for individual and group study. These include resources for Advent, Lent, Confirmation and the Decade of Evangelism.
Write or call now for a full list of publications:
The Bible Reading Fellowship
Peter's Way
Sandy Lane West
Oxford
OX4 5HG
Tel: 0865 748227

Our World, God's World

Readings, reflections and prayers on the environment

Barbara Wood

OPENING THE BIBLE

Text copyright © Barbara Wood 1986

The author asserts the moral right
to be identified as the author of this work

Published by
The Bible Reading Fellowship
Sandy Lane West, Oxford, England
ISBN 0 7459 2307 0
Albatross Books Pty Ltd
P O Box 320, Sutherland, NSW 2232, Australia
ISBN 0 7324 0637 4

First published 1986
This edition 1992
All rights reserved

Unless otherwise acknowledged, Scripture quotations are from
The Jerusalem Bible © Darton, Longman & Todd Ltd and
Doubleday and Company Inc. 1966, 1967 and 1968.

A catalogue record for this book is available
from the British Library

Printed and bound by Cox & Wyman Ltd, Reading

Contents

Foreword by David Bellamy

Introduction

*For children everywhere, especially
Catherine, Ben, Anna-Marie, Sebastian,
Felix, Sophie and all my godchildren.
It will be their world tomorrow.*

Foreword

by David Bellamy

God's first commandment to people was to have dominion over all living things, all the plants and the animals. Why? one must ask. Why, because their diverse populations make up the life support system of Space Ship Earth. Life support systems which:

maintain the fertility of the soils,

cleanse rivers, lakes and seas,

maintain the levels of oxygen and carbon dioxide in living balance in the atmosphere,

water the dry earth with pure sweet rain,

maintain the genetic diversity of life.

Take away the plants, take away the animals, destroy the forests and slowly but surely those life support systems run down and people start to die of starvation and environmental pollution.

As you think about God's world, let these facts sink into your mind:

1. One third of the world's population lives under the constant threat of malnutrition.

2. 28 children under the age of 5 die of conditions relating to malnutrition and environmental pollution every minute.

3. One third of the world's arable land surface is at risk of becoming a desert because of human misuse, much of which is funded by rich countries.

4. The world is losing at least 50 hectares of natural and semi-natural vegetation every minute of every day.

5. The world is losing at least one species of plant and animal a day and the rate of extinction is increasing. By the end of the century it is estimated that 1.25 million species will have become extinct thanks to the profligate misuse of this planet by mankind.

Where in all this is 'dominion'?

The thinking world is looking for new leadership to lead a green revolution back to the pathways of righteousness towards true dominion.

God has set us an awesome, immense task. Is the Christian church really up to the challenge?

Please read this book, follow its directives, and pray that the church will be up to that task for the sake of God's creation.

God's grandeur

The world is charged with the grandeur of God.
  It will flame out, like shining from shook foil;
  It gathers to a greatness, like the ooze of oil
Crushed. Why do men then now not reck his rod?
Generations have trod, have trod, have trod;
  And all is seared with trade; bleared, smeared with toil;
  And wears man's smudge and shares man's smell: the soil
Is bare now, nor can foot feel, being shod.

And for all this, nature is never spent;
  There lives the dearest freshness deep down things;
And though the last lights off the black West went
  Oh, morning, at the brown brink eastward, springs—
Because the Holy Ghost over the bent
  World broods with warm breast and with ah! bright wings.

Gerard Manley Hopkins

Introduction

Since the publication of the original version of *Our World, God's World*, which was tailored to those wishing to prepare for the feast of Christmas, books on the environment have become somewhat of a growth industry. Almost every week another appears with some new slant on the problems that face the living world. Some are scientific, others are full of beautiful pictures, and a few are theological.

This is not a new book. In the spirit of careful and sustainable use of the world's resources, which include spiritual insights, much of the content of this book has been recycled from the original version. What is new, however, is that I have adapted the reflections and added a few new ones so that the book can be used at any time during the year.

As this book is about renewing the face of the earth by examining our faith and the practice of our faith as that relates to our everyday life, I have also added some practical suggestions for action each day. Some of these are simple, others more ambitious. As each reader will have their own unique lifestyle and vocation not all the suggestions will be appropriate. They should be regarded as suggestions and not as rules which merely add to the burdens of life. Each person must start from where they are and adjust their life in a way appropriate to their own circumstances.

At the end of the day this is a book about our relationship with God and not about being 'green'. Being 'green' is not the same as being a Christian, although I firmly believe that those who truly live their lives serving and reverencing God quite unconsciously live in a way that is gentle and caring of creation.

I have also added some suggestions for discussion and worship at the end of each week for those who are using the book in a group. Some of these need a little preparation by the participants and so it might be helpful at each meeting to look ahead to the next week's worship and bear the suggestions in mind during the week's study.

Thanks are due to a number of people who made this revision possible. My husband Don, and my children, have not only put up with domestic chaos, but have remained cheerful and encouraging. Thanks, too, to Annie and Chris Stephens without whose cottage I would never have got the quiet and space I needed to reflect and pray about my work.

Barbara Wood

Psalm references are to the Jerusalem Bible. Bracketed numbers indicate other versions (RSV, NIV etc.)

All royalties from the sale of this book will go to organizations working to save the environment and alleviate poverty.

All the bulleted facts are taken from material produced by Friends of the Earth, Greenpeace and Traidcraft unless otherwise acknowledged.

1 The Purpose of Creation

Week 1: Day 1	Beginnings

Reading: *John 1:1–5, 9, 14*

In the beginning was the Word: the Word was with God and the Word was God. He was with God in the beginning. Through him all things came to be, not one thing had its being but through him. All that came to be had life in him and that life was the light of men, a light that shines in the dark, a light that darkness could not overpower...

The Word was the true light that enlightens all men; and he was coming into the world...

The Word was made flesh, he lived among us, and we saw his glory, the glory that is his as the only Son of the Father, full of grace and truth.

Christianity can be summed up in one startlingly simple statement: that God became man. This claim is unique among world religions. Christians do not believe that God came to visit us, that he disguised himself as a man. No. We believe that he became fully, humanly man, that he lived on earth, learnt a trade and worked for his living, was subject to temptations, had normal desires and passions, normal needs for food and sleep, the same capabilities for enjoyment and the same ability to feel and identify with pain and suffering as anyone else.

The difference was that this man Jesus, like us in every other way, did not submit to the temptations we all feel. He did not sin and so was able to take our sin and failure on himself and become the means for our salvation (Hebrews 2:17, 18).

This is a quite extraordinary claim and must seem scandalous to those who have not heard and understood the 'message of the truth and the good news of our salvation' (Ephesians 1:13). Why should the Word, as St John calls him, through whom all things had their being, the Word who was God, become flesh and subject himself to the vulnerability of human birth and the ignominy of the lonely death of a condemned man? 'His state was divine, yet he did not cling to his equality with God but emptied himself to assume the condition of a slave, and became as men are; and being as all men are, he was humbler yet, even to accepting death, death on a cross' (Philippians 2:6–8).

Why should this humiliation of our God be called Good News?

It is Good News because it gives meaning and purpose to our everyday life. When God became man in Jesus his Son he came to share our life, and in doing so he made the ordinariness of it holy. Jesus came to meet us on our own ground. He does not sit in heaven while we struggle to meet him, striving by our good works to gain acceptance and love. He, himself, came down to us, out of love, in the world he created out of love, to meet us in our human condition. He came because, from the beginning it was God's plan to 'bring everything together under Christ, as head, everything in the heavens and everything on earth' (Ephesians 1:10).

By coming into the world Jesus showed us that everyday life is holy. God gave us life and made us with material needs. He provides us with everything necessary to fulfil those needs. Jesus came to show us how to live with those needs and how to make them part of our relationship with him and with God the Father. Because Jesus came to be one of us, every part of our life comes together in him. Our material life, our intellectual life and our spiritual life are all part and parcel of the means by which we love and serve God. St John reminds us that Jesus, the Word, was there at the beginning, participating in creation. In becoming part of his creation by becoming man, Jesus underlines and re-emphasises a truth which was there from the beginning: that creation is holy, that everything on earth is made by God and sanctified by him. St John expresses this unity profoundly and beautifully: 'In the beginning was the Word . . . Through him all things came to be, not one thing had its being but through him . . . The Word was made flesh, he lived among us.'

The coming of God into the world resolves a great tension in which we are caught. We feel torn between the demands of the material world of which we are part and on which we depend for life, and the demands of the spiritual world towards which we strive and for which we long. The demands of everyday living often rob us of the time and peace of mind to spend on matters of God. Today's

14

reading sets us straight. The coming of Jesus brings these worlds together. To live in wholeness and holiness means to make everyday life part of our relationship with God. It means bringing together our fragmented lives so that Jesus can be born and live in us, and can direct our energies and purpose towards the coming of his kingdom, here on earth and in the life to come.

Prayer

Lord, you have made me body, mind and spirit. Often these parts of me seem to pull in different directions leaving no room for you. Be my centre, Lord, so that I may become whole.

Action

Choose one chore and as you do it each day pray: Glory be to the Father and to the Son and to the Holy Spirit, as it was in the beginning, is now and ever shall be, world without end. Alleluia.

Week 1: Day 2	Look up, your redemption is at hand

Reading:　　　　　　　　　*Luke 21:25–28*

There will be signs in the sun and moon and stars; on earth nations in agony, bewildered by the clamour of the ocean and its waves; men dying in fear as they await what menaces the world, for the powers of heaven will be shaken. And then they will see the Son of Man coming in a cloud with power and great glory. When these things begin to take place, stand erect, hold your heads high, because your liberation is near at hand.

In Isaiah 45:19 God says, 'I, Yahweh, speak with directness, I express myself with clarity.' Today's reading is an example of such direct simplicity. We are directed to watch for the 'signs'—world-wide and earth-shattering. When these come about then our liberation is at hand. Christ is here and we are called to lift up our heads and look up from our daily concerns which blind and preoccupy us, so that we can see him.

These signs are about us now, calling us to see Christ, not in the clouds of heaven, but here on earth. The persistent and re-occurring famine in Africa, the war zones of the Middle East, terrorist attacks, man-made disasters such as the nuclear accident at Chernobyl in 1986, chemical accidents like Bhopal in India, the poisoning of the Rhine and water supplies in the west country in England, the unknown effects of global warming and the hole in the ozone layer, and the continued threat of nuclear war and accident which, as the Knox translation of the Bible puts it, makes people 'wither away for fear', all these seem to be portents signalling the end of the world.

But for us their meaning lies not in their possible portents but in their actual call to respond to Christ now. Jesus comes to us in all these disasters, calling us to feed, shelter and clothe him, to bind his wounds, comfort him and follow his call for peace and reconciliation. Now as never before, events in the world are calling out to us as Christians to recognize and respond to Jesus in all these different guises.

It is when we recognize and respond to Jesus that our world becomes transformed and the vision of the world to come, which the prophets of both the Old and New Testaments give us, becomes reality. When we recognize Jesus in our midst then, as the prophet Isaiah says:

> Once more there will be poured on us the spirit from above; then shall the wilderness be fertile land and fertile land become forest. In the wilderness justice will come to live and integrity in the fertile land; integrity will bring peace, justice give lasting security.
> (Isaiah 32:15–17)

This passage in Isaiah is preceded by very different images. Before this outpouring of the spirit there are failing harvests and famine, fertile land falls into wasteland and the cities are deserted. Isaiah too was calling the people to see a new opportunity to embrace the word of God in the disasters they experienced. In the same way Jesus does not say, 'When these things come to pass hang your heads in despair, you are getting what you deserve.' He tells us to lift our heads and face the problems squarely, in the knowledge that he is there in the midst of them.

Facing problems can be painful. It demands a degree of honesty which we would rather avoid. It demands a response which may drastically affect our lives and our faith. The call Jesus gave seemed to be so simple: 'Follow me.' But that, as the disciples soon discovered, was where the simplicity ended. After that they were confused and bewildered by what Jesus said and did, some of which seemed contradictory, all of which left some people feeling uncomfortable.

The same contradictions appear when we respond to the problems that face our world. We are tempted to try and find a simple way out. We look for scapegoats. Or we simply try and throw money at it. And when that doesn't work we despair and come to the conclusion that the problems are so complex that only experts and specialists can solve them. Either way we remain uninvolved.

But to follow Jesus means to become involved. It means listening to him speaking to us in the events of the world as well as through his words in scripture. St John knew the difference between the world as it is and the world as it should be was whether or not the presence of the Lord was recognized and acknowledged. The world into which Jesus was born was full of sin. 'He was in the world that had its being through him, and the world did not know him' (John 1:10). The world to come, in which there will be harmony, peace and plenty, is one in which the presence of the Lord makes all the difference. 'Here God lives among men. He will make his home among them; they shall be his people, and he will be their God, his name is God-with-them' (Revelation 21:3).

Look up, lift your heads, your liberation is at hand. Jesus is here amongst us asking to be recognized and served. We must keep watch that we do not miss him when he comes to meet us. We can be sure of one thing: if we do not see him in the people around us we may never find him.

Prayer

Lord Jesus, open my eyes and my heart to recognize you wherever you are to be found.

Action

Reflect on the difference between opening your eyes and opening your heart. Think of someone you have seen in need. Bring them into your prayer and ask God to open your heart to their particular need. Keep watch for the answer so that you can act on it when it comes.

◆ *He who shuts his ear to the poor man's cry shall himself plead and not be heard.*
(Proverbs 21:13)

17

Reading: Isaiah 45:18, 19

Yes, thus says Yahweh, creator of the heavens who is God, who formed the earth and made it, who set it firm, created it no chaos but a place to be lived in: 'I am Yahweh, unrivalled, I have not spoken in secret in some corner of a darkened land. I have not said to Jacob's descendants, "Seek me in chaos". I, Yahweh, speak with directness, I express myself with clarity.'

Today's reading is one of many in the Bible in which the knowledge of God as Creator is firmly asserted. I chose this one in preference to others such as Genesis 1 or Psalm 104 [103] because in this passage from Isaiah God himself reminds us that 'I, Yahweh, speak with directness, I express myself with clarity.' The question of how the world came into being is of such importance that God himself clearly and unambiguously reminds us of it whenever sin causes us to deny or forget that he is the Creator of everything.

Everything we do and believe rests on this knowledge that the earth is the Lord's and the work of his hands. The creed begins with the words, 'I believe in one God, the Father, the Almighty, maker of heaven and earth, of all that is, seen and unseen.' Everything else follows on from that assertion.

The problem for Christians today is that we are not sure what this really means any more. In trying to discover how the world came into being we have come in danger of losing our belief that it was deliberately and consciously created. It has become difficult to read the first chapter of Genesis with an open, listening heart because in the background of our minds is the theory (which has been taught to us in childhood as fact) that everything came into being by chance, accident and as the result of adaptation to changing surroundings and the need to survive.

This has profound implications for our view of God and the living world, which in turn affects our relationship with God and his creation. For if we do not accept the God shown to us at the beginning but substitute a god of our own making, we end up by having a relationship with something other than the true God.

If we see a world around us that has come about by chance and accident then God becomes remote and uninvolved with creation. If we see living creatures as the result of the survival of the fittest, at the expense of the weak, then God becomes the God of the strong and not a God of love who cares for all his creatures, especially the weak and vulnerable. Gradually our view of God becomes distorted and we act accordingly. Creation is no longer holy, every part being desired and loved by God. It becomes something to be used and discarded. The weak and defenceless become despised and redundant except in their use to the strong and powerful.

Everything in the Bible from Genesis 1 onwards tells us that God created the world deliberately and consciously. 'In the beginning God created the heavens and the earth' (Genesis 1:1). He called everything there is into being and perfection. 'God said, "Let there be light" and there was light . . . God said, "Let dry land appear." And so it was . . . God said, "Let the earth produce vegetation . . ." And so it was . . . God made the two great lights . . . God said, "Let the waters teem with living creatures . . ." And so it was . . . God said, "Let the earth produce every kind of living creature . . ." And so it was.' Everything God made had purpose and after every outburst of creation 'God saw that it was good'. He wanted it to exist and he still wants it to exist because God is life and God is love. Without him nothing can remain in existence or have life. 'He spoke, and it was created; he commanded, and there it stood' (Psalm 33 [32]:9).

God has endowed humanity with an enquiring mind. Our desire to understand how the universe came about is one of his gifts and, as all his gifts, is given to help us to discover more about the Creator and his infinite love for us. But when we lose sight of God in our desire to understand, and try to explain the wonders of the world without him, we find ourselves on dangerous ground.

As we have lost our belief in God as creator, so the goodness of his creation has escaped us. But God continues to repeat his message even today and as we learn that to harm his creation is to harm ourselves, he is asking us to look afresh at his creation and his love for it.

Today's reading demands a new act of faith that God is indeed the Creator of all. If we accept this and accept that all that he has made is good, then we can make the prophetic visions of the restoration of harmony and fruitfulness of yesterday's reflection our own.

Earth's crammed with heaven
And every common bush afire with God!
But only he who sees takes off his shoes.
The rest sit round it and pick blackberries.
Elizabeth Barrett Browning, *Aurora Leigh*

Prayer
Lord, as we reflect upon your glorious creation, may our eyes behold and rejoice; may we listen and be glad (*Service of the Heart*).

Action
Read Genesis 1:1–15 slowly, asking God to open your eyes and heart to

see his love, goodness and purpose in his creation.

◆ *Each day between 3 and 50 species of life become extinct. By AD2000 15–20% of all species on earth may have disappeared due to human activities. That is, about 1,000,000 species will have become extinct.*
WWF Network, *The New Road*

◆ *At least 20,000 plants have edible parts and of these 3,000 have at some time or other been used as a food supply by different human communities. Today we depend on about 20 plant species and 10 animal species for our food.*
WWF Network, *The New Road,* **Jul–Sept 1990**

Week 1: Day 4   Creation speaks of God

Reading: Psalm 19:1–4

The heavens declare the glory of God, the vault of heaven proclaims his handiwork; day discourses of it to day, night to night hands on the knowledge.
No utterance at all, no speech, no sound any one can hear; yet their voice goes out throughout the earth, and their message to the ends of the world.

When my children were small they were forever drawing, writing and making things. Invariably they would give me the fruits of their labours as a present. I still have many of these gifts of love: sculptures on the mantelpiece, love letters secreted away in books, and a simple wooden crucifix bearing the marks of painstaking planing and sanding and a little finger mark where the cross was held as it was being varnished. Each one of these gifts contains something of the child who gave it to me and reminds me of their particular personality and interests.

Whatever we craft or make ourselves contains something of us. It bears our stamp. So it should not surprise us that creation speaks to us of its Creator. 'Every work that he does is full of glory and majesty' (Psalm 111:3). Throughout the Old Testament there is a deep consciousness that creation speaks of God and reflects his glory. Hymns of praise testify to the wonders of God's creation. Deep religious truths are seen in the context of the material world. This is not merely poetic expression. It is the recognition that one of the ways of knowing God is to look at his handiwork. 'The heavens declare the glory of God, the vault of heaven proclaims his handiwork,' says the Psalmist.

If we look at the world around us in this light we will learn something of God. We can glimpse something of his beauty in each flower, his care and love in the way nature provides for all our needs, 'All creatures depend on you to feed them throughout the year; you provide the food they eat, with generous hand you satisfy their hunger' (Psalm 104 [103]:27, 28). We can see his perfection in the extraordinary complexity and intricacy of the design of the universe and in the way everything is interrelated and interconnected. We glimpse something of his awesome strength in the powerful forces of nature, in the wind, in earthquakes, volcanoes and the strength of the seas; and of his gentleness in the caressing breeze rustling through new leaves in spring. As we look into the stars and contemplate what lies beyond we glimpse the incomprehensible nature of the infinite.

No one saw this better than St Francis of Assisi. He recognized the hand of God in everything and used this knowledge for never ending reflection and worship of his Creator. 'He could never bear to put out lanterns or candles because they reminded him of the Light of the World, and when he washed his hands he chose a place where the water that fell could not be trodden on by his feet, for water was a symbol of penitence. When he walked over stones he walked in reverence for love of him who is called the Rock, and he never would allow a whole tree to be cut down for firewood because Christ died on a tree' (Elizabeth Goudge, *St Francis of Assisi*).

An attitude like St Francis shows us how the created world can lead us to God at every moment. He is present in everything he has made and speaks to us through it. As Thomas Merton writes: 'Creation had been given to man as a clean window through which the light of God could shine into men's souls. Sun and moon, night and day, rain, the sea, the crops, the flowering tree, all these things were transparent. They spoke to man not of themselves only but of Him who made them' (*Bread in the Wilderness*).

Prayer
The whole creation speaks thy praise ... that so our soul rises out of its mortal weariness unto thee, helped upwards by the things thou hast made, and passing beyond them unto thee who hast wonderfully made them; and there refreshment is and strength unfailing (St Augustine).

Action
Find some natural object—a stone, a flower, a leaf, a picture of a landscape, animal or bird, and use it as the focus of your prayer to discover the presence of God in the world around you.

21

Reading: *Psalm 8:1–9*

Yahweh, our Lord, how great your name throughout the earth!
Above the heavens is your majesty chanted by the mouths of
children, babes in arms. You set your stronghold firm against your
foes to subdue enemies and rebels.
I look up at your heavens, made by your fingers, at the moon and
stars you set in place— ah, what is man that you should spare a
thought for him, the son of man that you should care for him.
Yet you have made him little less than a god, you have crowned him
with glory and splendour, made him lord over the work of your
hands, set all things under his feet,
sheep and oxen, all these, yes, wild animals too, birds in the air,
fish in the sea travelling the paths of the ocean.
Yahweh, our Lord, how great your name throughout the earth!

What an extraordinary mystery this psalm invites us to ponder. After God has
made the heavens and the earth in perfection he creates man and woman—
different from all the other creatures he has made, 'little less than a god...
crowned with glory and splendour.' But man and woman were no after-
thought. They were central to God's purpose of creation. 'Before the world
was made, he chose us, chose us in Christ, to be holy and spotless, and to live
through love in his presence' (Ephesians 1:4).

This, therefore, is the purpose of creation: to enable us to live in love in
God's presence. This is the answer to the question the Psalmist poses: 'Ah,
what is man that you should spare a thought for him, the son of man that you
should care for him?' God's love for us is no passing thought or fancy. He
created us, in his image, that is with all the qualities he himself possesses, to
live in his creation, and with it and through it, to live with him and share his
love.

This imprint of God is still with us. Those qualities with which he endowed us
are those we need to live in love, and those which we can see perfectly in Jesus
Christ, God made man. 'Like us in all things but sin.' This is why it is so
important to study carefully everything Jesus said and did because he reveals to
us not only what God is like but what we ourselves are like when sin is removed.

Creation, too, reveals these qualities to us. St Paul tells us that there is no
excuse for anyone not to know God because he is to be seen in everything he has
made. 'Ever since God created the world his everlasting power and deity—
however invisible— have been there for the mind to see in the things he has

22

made' (Romans 1:20). In nature we see perfection, beauty, order, generous provision for the needs of every creature in food, shelter, protection and living space. We see the constant forgiveness and renewal as nature adjusts to the abuses of humankind.

Pascal said, 'Nature has some perfections to show that she is the image of God; and some defects, to show that she is only the image' (*Pensées*). We see God reflected in nature, but nature is not God. Unlike God nature is not infinite. Her resources are not infinite, her levels of tolerance are not unlimited. The delicate balance that maintains life, while amazingly forgiving and adaptable, has its limits. Balance is maintained when the purpose of creation is maintained and God's creatures live in love and care for each other because they are living in love with God. But as soon as this purpose is forgotten then the balance is upset.

The Psalmist put his whole reflection on the place of man within the splendour of creation in the context of the greatness of God, framing his meditation with the words, 'Yahweh, our Lord, how great your name throughout the earth.' When we acknowledge this to be primary then we are facing God and allowing his image to become imprinted on us. Then we see the rest of his creation with his eyes as a sign of his love—more than a sign—a manifestation of an incomprehensible love, because this gift contains more than we will discover in our lifetime and yet he gives it all to us. When we face God and reflect him then we turn away from ourselves and our desires and wants. Our selfish desires make us see creation merely as the source of fulfilling our wants, as the means towards satisfying our craving for comfort, wealth and an easy life. Being 'lord over the work of his hands' does not mean exploiting it but caring for it and loving it as he does.

Jesus had strong words to say about those who took advantage of and abused the power they had been given by their master. In the parable of the conscientious steward (Matthew 24:45–51), the steward who beats his fellow servants and becomes a glutton and a drunkard in his master's absence will be taken by surprise when his master comes home. 'The master will cut him off and send him to the same fate as the hypocrites, where there will be weeping and grinding of teeth.'

Prayer
Holy, holy, holy, Lord, God of power and might,
Heaven and earth are full of your glory.
Hosanna in the highest.

Reflection
Imagine you are a being from another world. You are told that

humankind is made in the image of its God. That God is the Creator of all there is on earth. What would you deduce about God by observing the actions of those made in his image towards his creation? Do you believe in such a God?

Week 1: Day 6   Man's partnership with God

Reading: *Genesis 2:15–22*

Yahweh God took the man and settled him in the garden of Eden to cultivate and take care of it. Then Yahweh God gave the man this admonition, 'You may eat indeed of all the trees in the garden. Nevertheless of the tree of the knowledge of good and evil you are not to eat, for on the day you eat of it you shall most surely die.' Yahweh God said, 'It is not good that the man should be alone. I will make him a helpmate.' So from the soil Yahweh fashioned all the wild beasts and all the birds of heaven. These he brought to the man to see what he would call them; each one was to bear the name the man would give it. The man gave names to all the cattle, all the birds of heaven and all the wild beasts. But no helpmate suitable for man was found for him. So Yahweh God made the man fall into a deep sleep. And while he slept, he took one of his ribs and enclosed it in flesh. Yahweh God built the rib he had taken from the man into a woman, and brought her to the man.

In the first account of creation man and woman are created in the image of God and given lordship over creation. Some have seen this as an explanation and justification for all the human race has done to exploit the earth and its resources. This is certainly so if we see ourselves as being made in the image of a God who has the power to create or destroy, a ruthless God interested only in pleasing himself. But the second account of creation gives another dimension to being master. 'Cultivate and take care.' God has given us the whole of the earth to use, to develop, to tame, to cultivate and *to care for*. This means to respect and to ensure that the fine balance and beauty of nature is not upset by thoughtless exploitation. It means that the right use is made of the earth's resources so that the whole of mankind can live in dignity.

Today's reading is the picture of a loving gardener for whom work is a pleasure, who loves and knows his plants and their needs. He treats them with utmost tenderness so that they can grow to display their beauty to its loveliest and their fruitfulness to its utmost. His work is that of enablement, allowing the garden to fulfil its potential; ensuring that the soil is cared for so that the plants can bear fruit. God did not intend that we should sit back and do nothing. He himself is Creator and we were made in his image. He intends us to use our creative nature in the way we use his gifts to live on the earth. It is part of his plan for mankind and the means by which we reflect his glory. 'The sun rises ... and man goes out to work, and to labour until dusk. Yahweh, what variety you have created, arranging everything so wisely' (Psalm 104 [103]:22–24).

Work is not the consequence of sin but divinely instituted so that we become participants in the creative process. It is more than a means to obtaining the basic necessities of life; it is an act of prayer; it is the means by which we grow towards God; it is the means by which we grow towards and work out our relationship with others. Let us not forget that Adam and Eve were partners, helpmates, one flesh in the enterprise God handed to them.

The difficulties we encounter in serving and glorifying God in our work are the consequences of sin. It is sin that forces many people to toil in unfulfilling, unpleasant work. It is sin of horrifying dimensions when one looks at the numbers of people who do boring, repetitive work that destroys their humanity. We cause and prolong sin every time we buy or use something that requires this kind of toil from our brothers and sisters.

The consequences of sin penetrate the workplace at a very deep level. Our participation in the creative process takes place every time we are involved in transforming the resources of the earth into those things we need and use, whether in finance, management, selling or in the production process itself. Yet much of this work today is clearly not serving and glorifying God in that it leads directly or indirectly to harming or even destroying the earth through pollution, waste and interference in the ecosystem. What are we to do? We are enmeshed in sin and trapped by something larger than ourselves. Even if we would prefer to work elsewhere we are not always able to find a less harmful way of earning our living.

Everyone in this situation is sharing in the sin of the world and therefore sharing in the cross of Christ. Our first task is to face that and accept the pain as Christ did, knowing that pain is not God's will but that he accepted it out of love. There is pain in the fact that we are involved in sin and pain in the knowledge that others suffer because of us and that creation suffers because of us. Christ can use that pain if we offer it to him each day. It will become our source of strength to show our love for God and his gifts in new and creative ways within our workplace and in our personal lives.

Prayer

God of our ancestors, Lord of mercy, who by your word have made all things, and in your wisdom have fitted man to rule the creatures that have come from you, to govern the world in holiness and justice and in honesty of soul to wield authority, grant me Wisdom, consort of your throne, and do not reject me from the number of your children.
(Wisdom 9:1–4)

Action

Begin a balance sheet. Put on the credit side all those activities in which you are participating in God's creative activity. On the debit side put those activities which are destructive and harmful. Put the list before God in prayer and ask him to help you discover ways of reducing the debits and increasing the credits. Decide on one debit that you are going to get rid of. Keep the list and adjust it throughout these reflections as you become aware of new ways in which you can share in God's partnership or in which you are sinning against it.

Debit

◇ 1. Using the car for short journeys

◇ 2. Buying packaged food

◇ 3. Putting on the heating while wearing a T-shirt

Credit

◇ 1. Using a bike or walking

◇ 2. Using my own durable shopping bags

◇ 3. Composting all waste vegetable matter

Week 1: Day 7   **The unity of creation at Bethlehem**

Reading: *Luke 2:6–16*

While they were there the time came for her to have her child, and she gave birth to a son, her first-born. She wrapped him in swaddling clothes, and laid him in a manger because there was no room for them at the inn. In the countryside close by there were shepherds who lived in the fields and took it in turns to watch their flocks during the night. The angel of the Lord appeared to them and the glory of the Lord shone round them. They were terrified, but the angel said, 'Do not be afraid. Listen, I bring you news of great joy, a joy to be shared by the whole people. Today in the town of David a saviour has been born to you, he is Christ the Lord. And here is a sign for you: you will find a baby wrapped in swaddling clothes and lying in a manger.' And suddenly with the angel there was a great throng of the heavenly host, praising God and singing: 'Glory to God in the highest heaven, and peace to men who enjoy his favour.' Now when the angels had gone from them into heaven, the shepherds said to one another, 'Let us go to Bethlehem and see this thing that has happened which the Lord has made known to us.' So they hurried away and found Mary and Joseph, and the baby lying in the manger.

St Luke gives us a beautiful picture of the unity of the divine and human which takes place at the birth of Jesus. The whole of creation is present in all its forms, drawn together at this moment of God's entry into his creation. There is the straw and the wood of the manger, the animals, the human presence of Mary and Joseph and, if we add the account of St Matthew, the star shining above. One might say the four levels of creation were brought together for the birth of Jesus through whom they were all made. Finally, together with inanimate creation, plant life, animal life and human life, is the presence of the angelic host, confirming by their words 'glory to God in the highest heaven and peace to men' (on earth) that salvation is to be found in the coming together of heaven and earth in Jesus.

The presence of the different stages of creation at the manger brings everything around us into God's plan for our salvation. At the birth of Christ we are brought face to face with the holiness of all aspects of life. It is a spiritual event that transforms the material world.

This brings our striving for holiness right down to a practical everyday level. The way we use creation is part of our relationship with God and path to him. Everything we do becomes part of our response to God's invitation to enter into a loving relationship with him. 'Everything' means our daily, humdrum life because everything we do impinges in some way on God's creation. Everything we need for daily life comes from the raw materials which God has provided, so using them properly is an act of reverence, gratitude and love.

Today, as we meditate on the scene which St Luke describes for us, we should try to visualize ourselves there too. We are part of God's creation brought together to worship Jesus and see to his needs. Each part has a unique role to play in salvation and is therefore of inestimable value to us because it is our salvation.

If we are to respond to God's invitation to a relationship with him through Jesus then we have to consider too our relationship towards everything he loves and considers precious. We have to examine our attitude towards the whole of creation; towards nature, resources, animals and people. This is hard work, as we will find that our minds are clouded by our attachment to all the things we want for ourselves. These can be material wants and desires, our position in life, our friends, our ambitions. Without knowing it we can put all these things between ourselves and God and allow our wants to obscure the part that creation plays in praising and worshipping its Creator, and the essential part it plays in enabling us to praise and worship our God and Creator and live in love with him.

Jesus came to liberate us from all those barriers which separate us from God. When he began his public ministry he announced that:

> *'The spirit of the Lord has been given to me, for he has anointed me. He has sent me to bring the good news to the poor, to proclaim liberty to captives and to the blind new sight, to set the downtrodden free, to proclaim the Lord's year of favour.'*
> **(Luke 4:18, 19)**

These words are directed at all of us—poor in understanding, captive by our attachments, blind to our responsibilities and impact on the world, oppressed by our failure to live the life God wants us to live. God knows this and in his love sends Jesus, the Saviour, Christ the Lord, our liberator.

Prayer
Lord Jesus, be born in me today so that heaven and earth can meet in everything I do.

Action
Think ahead to next Christmas. Consider the impact on God's creation that your plans might have. Will your presents be harmful to what he has made? Wrapping paper? Cards? What gifts could you make or grow yourself? Keep a look out for recycled cards and wrapping paper and gifts that also benefit charities. (Mail order from Oxfam, Traidcraft, Christian Aid, World Wide Fund for Nature, Greenpeace, Friends of the Earth, among others. See 'Useful addresses' at the back.)

28

Note to group leader: The aim of these questions is to bring out an awareness of our dependence on God for the basic necessities of life—fresh air, clean water, food from a healthy productive earth, the means by which we keep warm, etc. You may find that the discussion revolves around gifts such as love, friendship, intelligence, etc, because our material needs for life are taken for granted.

If the group is large enough, discuss the questions in groups of two or three and then share your answers and insights.

Useful props

1. Pencils and paper for those who feel unable to pray spontaneously and prefer to write their prayers first.
2. Objects from the natural world—at least as many as members of the group: e.g. stone, piece of wood, plant, vegetable, feather, glass of water; or something made that is beneficial and not harmful and shows our partnership with God in creation, e.g. spectacles, a hand tool, a woollen or cotton garment.
3. A candle (and matches) as a focus for the worship on a small table big enough to hold the natural objects.

Questions for discussion

1. For which of God's gifts are you the most grateful?
2. Could you live without them?
3. Would your answers mean anything to those less fortunate than yourself such as an Iraqi Kurd, one of the world's 800 million undernourished, or someone who lived around Chernobyl at the time of the accident? Why?
4. Do you see yourself as part of God's creation or outside/above it?
5. Discuss the week's suggestions for action. Have you tried to undertake any of these? Is there something you all feel able to undertake? Share your experience.

Preparation for worship

1. Invite each person to prepare a prayer of thanksgiving for those gifts of creation which mean most to them. Let them choose an object to symbolize these gifts.
2. Reflect together on the discussion. What else might you incorporate in your worship and bring before the Lord?

Suggestions for worship

◇ **Read Psalm 104 [103] slowly, pausing between each verse to** allow time to visualize the glories of creation and the praise to become heart felt.

◇ Let each person offer their prayer and lay their symbol on the table around the lighted candle.

◇ If the discussion has led to any practical decisions for action, offer these to the Lord and ask him to bless your efforts.

2 Who Is Obscuring God's Designs?

Week 2: Day 1   **Prophets**

Reading: *Jeremiah 5:23–25*

But this people has a rebellious, unruly heart; they have rebelled—being good at this! They have not said in their hearts: Come, we must fear Yahweh our God who gives the rain, the early rain and the later, at the right time of year, who assures us of weeks appointed for harvest. Your crimes have made all this go wrong, your sins have deprived you of these favours.

Environmentalists are often called prophets of doom. Their message essentially appears to be that the human race is heading for a collision-course with nature. They say that unless we completely re-think the economic basis on which our lives are run, disaster and destruction will result. We are relieved when others speak up and say that such gloomy predictions are unfounded and that science will find a way out. Such people tell us that the best solution to the world's problems is more economic growth, more production, more consumption, and greater exploitation of the world's resources. Such a course of action will ensure prosperity for all and, above all, peace.

Whom should we believe?

At the time of Jeremiah, the Jews were faced with a similar dilemma of whom to believe. Jeremiah was the prophet of doom. He told them plainly that their godless lives would lead to the destruction of their way of life and the fertility of their land. 'Your crimes have made all this go wrong.' As soon as he began his ministry he was shouted down by others who claimed to be prophets and told the people that everything was fine and that Jeremiah was mad. It turned out, of course, that these were false prophets, lulling the people into a false sense of security and encouraging them to close their ears to Jeremiah's authentic message and call to repentance.

Jeremiah was not the only Old Testament prophet who condemned these false prophets, who are always trying to lead the people of God astray. In Micah we read: 'Yahweh says this against the prophets who lead my people astray: So long as they have something to eat they cry "Peace". But on anyone who puts nothing into their mouths they declare war' (Micah 3:5). Amos adds, 'You think to defer the day of misfortune, but you hasten the day of violence' (Amos 6:3).

How is the authenticity of the prophets to be recognized? How do we know which voice speaks the words of God? It is important to know, first of all, which God these prophets claim to be worshipping. We need to recognize the 'Baals' of today's world. There must also be a unity between the way our prophets live and the message they preach. Their lives, as much as their words, testify to the truth. And the message itself will always contain the call to repentance and emphasize the love of God and his desire for reconciliation. If we were already reconciled there would be no need for the prophets.

Jeremiah did not merely preach death and destruction. Always there is this yearning of God for his people to return and respond to his love. 'Come back, disloyal Israel—it is Yahweh who speaks—I shall frown on you no more, since I am merciful—it is Yahweh who speaks. I shall not keep my resentment for ever. Only acknowledge your guilt:' (Jeremiah 3:12, 13). 'I have loved you with an everlasting love, so I am constant in my affection for you' (Jeremiah 31:3).

Finally, there is always a connection made between the spiritual life of the people and the effect this has on the material world. In other words, our way of life is part of the message and creation's response testifies whether it is of God or not.

The true prophet sees things as they really are. He interprets what is happening in the world and shows us where we have strayed from the true path. The purpose of his message is to lead us to repentance and change, so that we can find our proper place in the whole of God's creation and plan. If we wait for statistics to show us whether today's prophets are right after all, it may be too late! Israel had to experience the destruction of Jerusalem and the humiliation of the exile before they understood the word of Jeremiah.

The possibility of change, based on repentance, acknowledging our involvement in the ills of the world, gives testimony to the voice of God calling us today. He calls us to compassion, justice, trust, obedience, love. In that re-direction and our response—our recognition of God's unfathomable, unswerving love for us—lies our hope.

In the midst of the doom and destruction, when the false prophets despaired and were unable to give the people any hope of comfort, Jeremiah was able to direct Israel's vision beyond their troubles to God's wonderful promise to be fulfilled in the coming of Jesus. Lest the people should not hear him he repeats it twice, once in Jeremiah 23:5, 6 and then again in 33:14–16.

> See the days are coming—it is Yahweh who speaks—when I am going to fulfil the promise I made to the House of Israel and the House of Judah:
>
> *In those days and at that time, I will make a virtuous Branch grow for David, who shall practise honesty and integrity in the land. In those days Judah shall be saved and Israel shall dwell in confidence. And this is the name the city shall be called: Yahweh-our-integrity.*

They are words of hope, not the despair with which Jeremiah is so often associated. In the midst of the threats to our lives today, the coming of Jesus reminds us that God's wish for us is not destruction and death but salvation and life. Yet we must also remember that it was the people of God whose closed ears and hearts failed to respond to Jeremiah and therefore had to experience the suffering that came upon them. It was the people of God who failed to recognize the Son of God when he came, and so did not understand the message of salvation. Will the people of God today hear and understand?

Prayer
Give me ears to hear your word in the prophets of today, the wisdom to understand your message, and the courage to respond.

Action
Do you belong to an environmental pressure group such as Friends of the Earth, Greenpeace or the Worldwide Fund for Nature? How about asking for it as a Christmas or birthday present? Or could it be a present from you to someone you love? (See Useful Addresses at the back.)

Reading: *Romans 8:18–23*

I think that what we suffer in this life can never be compared to the glory, as yet unrevealed, which is waiting for us. The whole creation is eagerly waiting for God to reveal his sons. It was not for any fault on the part of creation that it was made unable to attain its purpose, it was made so by God; but creation still retains the hope of being freed, like us, from its slavery to decadence, to enjoy the same freedom and glory as the children of God. From the beginning till now the entire creation, as we know, has been groaning in one great act of giving birth; and not only creation, but all of us who possess the first-fruits of the Spirit, we too groan inwardly as we wait for our bodies to be set free.

For many years voices have been raised trying to direct our attention to what is happening to God's creation. Those who have ears to hear have looked on them as modern day prophets, for their message is essentially the same as that of the prophets of the Old Testament and John the Baptist. Both cry out: 'Repent! Change your ways, or the world as you know it will be destroyed.'

Now the voices of the prophets are being drowned by the great groan of creation itself, increasingly desperate to be released from the bondage that prevents it from attaining its purpose. Only this is not the groaning of giving birth, but the groan of death.

St Paul refers to 'the entire creation', and we are discovering that it is indeed the whole of creation that is affected by our sin. Hardly a day passes without some new evidence of the effects of our polluting way of life. At first it seemed that others could take the blame. Chemical accidents and oil spillages are clearly the responsibility of the industries concerned. We are appalled when the innocent suffer and are not readily compensated. At Seveso in Italy it was the unborn who suffered because the chemical released was known to cause birth abnormalities. Many women were advised to have abortions. At Bhopal in India, 2,000 died. Many more still suffer injuries and blindness, their suffering worsened by their poverty and powerlessness. When the Rhine was poisoned by chemicals accidentally discharged by a factory in Basle it was the fish and other river life that died. The Exxon Valdez disaster killed and maimed hundreds of sea birds and other marine life was coated with oil. The nuclear accident at Chernobyl still affects many with radiation sickness, and will be responsible for much suffering in the future as cancer takes its toll.

All these outraged or even frightened us, but at least we could identify the culprits and direct our wrath against them for damaging creation. We could demand that steps were taken to ensure that there were higher safety standards and that victims should be compensated. But creation is not groaning because of isolated accidents, however serious. It is afflicted in all its parts. The sweet rain is poisoned and, instead of giving life as it falls, kills trees and plants that are susceptible to its acidity. Thousands of square miles of forest have been devastated by acid rain all over the world: Scandinavia, Eastern and Western Europe, especially Germany, North America, the Far East. In Britain 66% of oaks, 57% of beech trees and 60% of yews were found damaged in 1988 (Greenpeace 1988). Fish are also extremely sensitive to acidity in rivers and ponds, and many waterways in affected areas are dead or dying as a result of acid rain. The air we breathe is no longer pure and fresh, but in some areas is so polluted that to breathe causes ill-health, asthmas and respiratory disease.

The earth, source of our nourishment, is so full of chemicals, pesticides, insecticides, herbicides and other agents of death that its fertility has become diminished and in many places the soil is impoverished and even lifeless.

The sun too is affected. Our source of light and warmth, so essential to all life, is becoming our enemy as the hole in the ozone layer lets in ultra-violet rays which endanger our health and damages those vitally important forms of life at the bottom of the food chain.

We cannot blame others for this suffering in creation. Nor can we blame God. It is not his wrath that is disfiguring what is good. It is our way of life that pollutes and destroys. Is it as Isaiah said?—

> *The earth is mourning, withering,*
> *the world is pining, withering.*
> *The heavens are pining away with the earth.*
> *The earth is defiled*
> *under its inhabitants' feet,*
> *for they have transgressed the law, violated the precept,*
> *broken the everlasting covenant.*

Is our way of life itself a violation of God's law? What had seemed to be a problem for specialists like scientists, industrialists, technologists, economists and governments to solve, now appears to be our problem because it relates to the way we live and use God's creation. The sickness we see in our natural environment is the manifestation of a process of disregard and violence towards God's creation, something which the prophets of old called sin against God, sin against the work of his hands, and disregard for his loving purpose for mankind. As St Paul says in today's passage, our spiritual liberation and that of the whole of creation is closely bound up and we have to look hard at ourselves, our place in creation, and our faith in God, our Creator and liberator, before we can begin to cooperate with him in the liberation of the whole of creation from the bonds of sin, death and decay.

Prayer
Lord God, the world is full of your glory and I have been blind. Now your glory is being veiled by my lack of care. Forgive me for my lack of concern in the past. Unstop my ears so that I hear the great groan of creation so afflicted by the thoughtlessness of mankind.

Action
Check through your cleaning agents. Discard all those which are environmentally unsafe, especially any aerosols using CFCs. Resolve to buy only environmentally safe ones in future even if it means more elbow grease from you to get the same sparkling effects.

◆ *Acid rain is caused mainly by sulphur dioxide and nitrogen oxides. Britain is the largest producer of these pollutants in Western Europe, and 'exports' much of it to the rest of Europe and Scandinavia.*

◆ *65% of sulphur dioxide comes from power stations.*

◆ *40% of nitrogen oxides come from power stations and 40% from traffic.*
Greenpeace

◆ *By the early 1980s, 5,000 lakes in Norway were suffering from acidification.*

◆ *40,000 of Sweden's 90,000 lakes are seriously acidified.*

◆ *At least 78 British waters are acidified or in danger.*

Reading: *John 4:6–10*

Jesus, tired by the journey, sat straight down by the well. It was about the sixth hour. When a Samaritan woman came to draw water, Jesus said to her, 'Give me a drink.' His disciples had gone into the town to buy food. The Samaritan woman said to him, 'What? You are a Jew and you ask me, a Samaritan, for a drink?'— Jews, in fact, do not associate with Samaritans. Jesus replied: 'If you only knew what God is offering and who it is that is saying to you: Give me a drink, you would have been the one to ask, and he would have given you living water.'

Today's reading is the beginning of a long exchange between Jesus and the Samaritan woman in which Jesus reveals that he is the Messiah. The scene is by a well at midday, the hottest time of the day. Their conversation is about water, a commonplace subject, appropriate to the time and place. But with Jesus the commonplace is holy and he uses this woman's understanding of the life-giving nature of water and her own thirst in the heat of the day to bring her to a new understanding of God and what he has to offer her through himself.

Throughout scripture water is used to bring people to a closer understanding of their need for God. Our need for God is like a parched throat in need of refreshing water. The Jews understood that life without water meant death. Their experience was that to obtain water to drink, for washing and for irrigating land was hard work and the sweet rain, when it came, was reason for profound gratitude and care. Only a fool would treat such a precious commodity in a wasteful way.

It can be hard for us to penetrate into the meaning of today's reading and the many wonderful references throughout scripture when our experience is so different. Since water has come into our homes we have ceased to value it and understand its life-giving qualities. We do not toil in the heat but merely turn on the tap. The extraordinary statement of Jesus that 'anyone who drinks the water I shall give him will never be thirsty again, the water I shall give will turn into a spring inside him' (verse 14), loses its meaning when we have a spring of water in our homes which we use primarily for our washing machines, dishwashers, garden sprinklers and car washing, preferring to quench our thirst with a can of fizzy drink or a cup of tea or coffee.

We no longer recognize water as necessary for life itself but rather as necessary to satisfy our desire for convenience and luxury. We do not just use water to grow our food and quench our thirst, but use it freely for all our production processes. Water is taken up from the ground and out of our rivers, used, and returned to run off into rivers and the sea taking with it many contaminants and pollutants. Through this process water is becoming, not the source of life but rather a threat to life. Heavily polluted rivers and seas cannot sustain life but kill the forms of life within them. In many parts of the world fish and marine life are found with tumours and lesions caused by pollutants. Other forms of life, such as seals, are falling prey to disease because their resistance has been lowered. Life in sea, river and lake is smothered by algae blooms caused by fertilizers and nitrates used by farmers, and ground water is contaminated. How can we understand the meaning of living water when water is becoming a possible source of danger? What can the cleansing water of baptism mean for us when water is polluted and contaminated?

Fortunately God, in his infinite love for us, does not tire of calling his people back to him and he can and will use the consequences of our way of life to teach us the truths to which our way of life blinds us. When Jesus said he was the 'living water' he was echoing God's words in Jeremiah (2:13). God accuses his people of having abandoned him 'the fountain of living water, only to dig cisterns for themselves, leaky cisterns that hold no water.' As we contemplate the dirty water with which we have replaced God's clean and sparkling gift to us we must, as the Samaritan woman did, face the truth about ourselves and our way of life. Then we can prepare to receive the Messiah, responding to John the Baptist's call to repent and be baptized in preparation for the one who is to come.

As we waste precious water and deplete the abundant sources which God has given us, we may learn to see again the meaning of Jesus's invitation to an ever-flowing spring of water within us.

Each time we wash our hands we have an opportunity to meditate on these things. Let us today thank God for water, repent for our participation in its misuse and reflect that the meaning of baptism is 'a pledge made to God from a good conscience' (1 Peter 3:21).

Prayer

'Praise be to my Lord for our sister water who is very serviceable unto us, humble and clean' (St Francis). May we learn to respect and love her so that we see again the goodness of God reflected in her depths.

Action

Become conscious of your water use. Every time you fill the kettle, flush the lavatory or use your dishwasher/washing machine put a small sum (2p or 5p) in a tin. Give the proceeds to CAFOD or Christian Aid to use for a project to bring water to a needy community.

◆ *The minimum water needed per day for a reasonable quality of life is 80 litres.*

◆ *Nearly $3/4$ of the world's population have access to only 50 litres per day.*

◆ *The average American uses up to 1,000 litres a day.*
Save the Earth

◆ *Failure to heed the signs of stress . . . could render as much as a fourth of the world's reliable (water) supply unsafe for use by the year 2000.*
World Watch Institute Report, 1985

◆ *1991 . . . North India—2,300 out of 2,700 wells have dried up.*

◆ *Beijing, China—$1/3$ of the cities' wells without water due to falling water table.*

◆ *USA—in some states water table is falling by about 1 metre a year.*
Save the Earth

Reading: *Matthew 13:31, 32*

He put another parable before them, 'The kingdom of heaven is like a mustard seed which a man took and sowed in his field. It is the smallest of all the seeds, but when it has grown it is the biggest shrub of all and becomes a tree so that the birds of the air come and shelter in its branches.'

Like water, the tree is a recurring symbol throughout the Old and New Testaments. The tree symbolizes strength, it signifies the presence of living water, it reflects the loving care of God in its provision of shelter, shade and food, and it is the symbol of our salvation in the form of the wooden cross. In today's reading we contemplate the miracle of the growth of this magnificent sign of the kingdom of God, encompassing all, sheltering all, caring for all.

In the Old Testament the destruction of trees is associated with God's wrath. We read in Daniel (chapter 4) about the vivid dream that so puzzled Nebuchadnezzar, in which the protective, life-giving tree is destroyed by God until the lessons of obedience to God's will and law have been learnt. Isaiah, too, warns that God will 'destroy the luxuriance of his forest and his orchard . . . the remnant of his forest trees will be so easy to count that a child could make the list' (Isaiah 10:18, 19).

The Old Testament writers knew well that the felling of trees resulted in desert. The Law of Moses has some specific references to the care and cultivation of trees (Leviticus 19:23–25), and expressly forbids their wholesale destruction in war. It is enshrined in the law of God that all useful trees, especially those which bear fruit, must be protected (Deuteronomy 20:19).

Again it seems that the prophecies are being fulfilled in our time (read Joel 2:3–5) and we are carrying out God's sentence with our own hands. Apart from the destruction of trees by acid rain and pollution, there is also deliberate, efficient destruction of the world's most beautiful and unique rainforests. The reasons vary from country to country but they have in common a ruthless determination to exploit the rainforests for quick gain.

In Central America it is largely to provide pasture for cattle destined for the American hamburger market. In Australia and the Far East it is to fill the ever-hungry paper mills of Japan. African hardwoods are used for our luxury buildings and furniture. After we have robbed the forests then those desperately poor people living on the edge of the forest add to our destruction as they look for fuel and a little patch of land from which to eke a miserable living. The UN Environment Programme has estimated that every minute at least 40 acres of tropical rainforest is destroyed by logging and burning. This is an annual area slightly larger than the United Kingdom.

The rainforests are unique and extraordinary habitats of the most abundant flora and fauna the world knows. Tropical rainforests cover 7% of the land surface of the earth yet they contain 50% of the world's species. As the rainforests disappear so do species of plant and animal life, many of which are not yet known to us. Unidentified, they are becoming extinct before they have been discovered and their purpose made known to humankind.

The real effect of this wholesale destruction of the primeval forest, perhaps the closest we can get today to the original creative outburst, is only slowly being realized. Some of it is still unknown. We know that within the tropical rainforest lies a vast genetic bank of countless strains and varieties of plant. Some of these are vital for future food supplies, containing genetic material which would enable disease resistant varieties, and high protein and other nutrient-bearing varieties, to be bred. If the earth's temperature is increasing through the greenhouse effect then this genetic material may become essential to adapt our food growing requirements to different climatic patterns.

Plants, too, contain the solutions to many of our medical problems. The tiny rose periwinkle was discovered just in time as the rainforest of Madagascar was being decimated. It contains a vital drug for the cure of childhood leukaemia. The range and scope of the secrets of the rainforests may remain forever known only to their Creator, never able to fulfil their role in his creative purpose if this destruction is not halted.

As inroads are made into the forest, the cleared land quickly ceases to be productive. Despite the lush and abundant growth of the rainforests, the soil is in fact among the poorest on earth. It is very thin, as the root systems of even the tallest trees are shallow because of the abundant rain, and the constant growth and decay provide the essential nutrients. Once cleared the soil quickly becomes exhausted and the thin layer of topsoil is blown or washed away by the rain. Without the trees the rain is no longer returned into the atmosphere and eventually drought becomes common. This is the tragic fate of Ethiopia, once green and lush. Today, of 40% forest covering that existed at the beginning of the century, only 4% remains.

How can we allow this destruction? As we ravage the earth, we become aware that God's creation is even more precious and more bountiful than we had ever imagined and yet we still fail to honour and respect it. The kingdom of heaven, the original garden of Eden, is contained in the wonders of the rainforests. Surely today we are seeing the prophecies of old fulfilled as a punishment for our ingratitude.

But if you do not listen to me, and do not observe each one of these

commandments, if you refuse my laws and disregard my customs . . . then I will deal in like manner with you . . . You shall sow your seed in vain . . . I will break your proud strength. I will give you a sky of iron, an earth of bronze. You shall wear out your strength in vain, your land shall not yield its produce any longer nor the trees their fruit.
(Leviticus 26:14–16, 19, 20)

Prayer
Lord Jesus, you died on a tree to give us life. Forgive us for destroying this symbol and supporter of life and help us to restore it to its true place in your creation.

Action
1. Buy and use as many Brazil nuts as possible. This encourages sustainable use of the tropical rainforest.
2. Put a sticker by your letter box saying 'Save Trees: No free newspapers or circulars thank you'. It works wonders.

◆ *Each year each person in Britain consumes an average of two trees worth of cardboard and paper.*

◆ *In the West the average person will consume more than 120 kg of paper a year. In the Third World only 8 kg per person is consumed.*
The Green Consumer Guide

◆ *95% of Britain's hardwood supplies come from badly managed and unsustainable sources.*
The Green Consumer Guide

◆ *15 million tons of pulp (1% of total pulp production) is thrown away each year in the form of disposable nappies.*
State of the World, 1991

Reading   *Exodus 16:4, 5*

Then Yahweh said to Moses, 'Now I will rain down bread for you from the heavens. Each day the people are to go out and gather the day's portion; I propose to test them in this way to see whether they will follow my law or not. On the sixth day, when they prepare what they have brought in, this will be twice as much as the daily gathering.'

In the first week of our reflections we focused on the abundance and generosity of God's creation and on his intention that mankind should reflect his loving care within that glory. This week we have begun to look at how we have failed. We see it from a spiritual perspective, but it is confirmed from a human point of view by economists and environmentalists. One such is Professor Barry Commoner who writes, 'Everywhere in the world there is evidence of a deep-seated failure in the effort to use the competence, the wealth, the power at human disposal for the maximum good of human beings. The environmental crisis is a major indication of this failure' (*The Closing Circle*).

Until the middle of this century no one had ever doubted that there was more than enough of everything in the world to go round. The ground was full of oil, coal, natural gas, minerals of every kind, forests were full of trees, the sea full of fish, vast areas of land remained unexploited for food production. Developing technology ensured that these abundant resources could be exploited and the kingdom of heaven seemed near to becoming heaven on earth.

Today a very different picture prevails. We are told that there is no longer enough to go round.

'Not enough' is not something we ever hear God saying. He is always the generous provider. The lack of gratitude of his people for their spectacular rescue from captivity in Egypt did not prevent God from providing manna and quails for them when it was needed in the wilderness. There was as much as they needed there every day.

Abundance and generosity are signs of God's presence; hoarding and greed are not. When the Israelites obeyed God, they were provided for; when they disobeyed, the manna went foul—a vivid sign of the effects of disobedience on our soul. (St Teresa of Avila is said to have had the extraordinary gift of smelling the state of a person's soul. Sinful people had such a foul stench that she could not bear them near her!)

It was the excess collected by the Israelites that went foul. It was a failure in

43

gratitude; it was lack of trust that God would provide again the following day; it was greed. We have our own stinking heaps of excess, the results of our own greed. Each year in the United Kingdom we produce nearly 150 million tons of industrial waste and 25 million tons of domestic waste. A large proportion of this could be re-used but it is easier in the short term to throw it away. In fact we have been educated towards this way of thinking for many decades. In 1929 Floyd Allen, a motor-car executive said, 'Advertizing is in the business of making people helpfully dissatisfied with what they have in favour of something better. The old factors of wear and tear can no longer be depended upon to create a demand. They are too slow.' (Quoted in Richard Foster, *Freedom of Simplicity*.)

This sort of attitude is directly opposed to the instructions God gave his people. He was trying to teach them that the concept of 'enough' is basic to proper living. This has not yet reached our understanding. Much of the talk about controlling pollution and waste is based upon trying to clean up existing processes. But these processes are geared to produce excess, to create new demands which result in a dissatisfaction with what one has and an imagined need to replace it. This creates pollution in itself. Moreover it is extremely costly. To reduce significantly the sulphur dioxide emissions on a plant producing 35,000 megawatts of power would cost some 5–10 million dollars. But to cut the requirements of energy by 35,000 megawatts would not only get rid of those sulphur dioxide emissions altogether, it would also cut carbon dioxide pollution and ozone pollution. And it would cost nothing. Alternatively, to cut this energy demand by increasing energy use efficiency would cost about one per cent of the 'cleaning up' method. Similar savings can be made by a different attitude to our rubbish. Much of what we discard can be re-used with great benefit to the environment. Think of the mountains of waste paper we throw away every day. Each ton of paper made from waste paper rather than new wood not only saves trees, it also saves between one third and one half of the energy required and reduces pollution by up to 95%.

Environmentalists talk about 'today's threats becoming tomorrow's catastrophes'. This week we have glimpsed some of the areas in which the threats are becoming dire. Today's reading leads us to the central truth about these economic and ecological problems. God provides for us amply, but written into his generosity is the concept of 'enough'. There is provision for feast-days, there is variety for all tastes, but not for greed or waste. Greed and waste are not compatible with a thankful heart and a loving stewardship. St Paul wrote to the Corinthians, 'People must think of us as Christ's servants, stewards entrusted with the mysteries of God. What is expected of stewards is that each one should be found worthy of his trust' (1 Corinthians 4:1, 2). These mysteries include the wonderful world he has made and all that is in it. It is time we took these words seriously.

Prayer

Yahweh my God, how great you are. All creatures depend on you to feed them throughout the year. You provide them with everything they require. With generous hands you satisfy all their needs.
(adapted from Psalm 104 [103]:27, 28)

Action

Phone your local council to discover your local recycling facilities. Find recycling containers to enable you to sort out your waste.

◆ *Recycled aluminium rather than virgin ore reduces:*
nitrogen oxide emissions by 95%,

◆ *sulphur dioxide emissions by 99%.*

◆ *Each ton of virgin copper ore produces 2.7 tons of sulphur oxide.*

◆ *In 1980 one third of copper smelted in Canada was recycled copper. Sulphur emissions were reduced by 1 million tons, which was equal to over one fifth of total sulphur dioxide emissions.*

◆ *Sulphur dioxide and nitrogen oxide emissions cause acid rain which kills trees, fish and other plant life.*

Week 2: Day 6   **Resources**

Reading: *Luke 16:1–8*

He also said to his disciples, 'There was a rich man and he had a steward who was denounced to him for being wasteful with his property. He called for the man and said, "What is this I hear about you? Draw me up an account of your stewardship because

45

you are not to be my steward any longer." Then the steward said to himself, "Now that my master is taking the stewardship from me, what am I to do? Dig? I am not strong enough. Go begging? I should be too ashamed. Ah, I know what I will do to make sure that when I am dismissed from office there will be some to welcome me into their homes." Then he called his master's debtors one by one. To the first he said, "How much do you owe my master?" "One hundred measures of oil" was the reply. The steward said, "Here, take your bond; sit down straight away and write fifty." To another he said, "And you, sir, how much do you owe?" "One hundred measures of wheat" was the reply. The steward said, "Here, take your bond and write eighty." The master praised the dishonest steward for his astuteness. For the children of this world are more astute in dealing with their own kind than are the children of light.'

This is a very difficult parable to understand because of its unexpected punchline. 'The master praised the dishonest steward for his astuteness.' The comments Jesus makes afterwards do not seem to enlighten us either. However, the parable seems to me to say a great deal about our situation in the world today.

We are the steward, caught being wasteful with the resources of the world with which we have been entrusted. Our careless and wasteful stewardship, which puts our own desires before the needs of the whole of God's family, is destroying these abundant resources and now we are in danger of losing what we have.

Our reaction is not to be sorry for our mismanagement. There is no contrition on the part of the dishonest steward; only thought for his own skin. How can he get out of the scrape he is in without deprivation or humiliation? He is not prepared to work hard (dig), nor suffer the disgrace of admitting his worthlessness by begging.

His course of action is like our own. He looks to others who still respect him for his position and makes use of their misfortunes to save his own skin. What is our reaction to the world crisis? It is not to pull our belts in, to acknowledge our share of responsibility for the starving and share what we have with them, it is not to adjust our lifestyles, to change our production and consumption patterns so that the depletion of resources is slowed down. Such a course of action is tantamount to admitting we have gone wrong; it would involve work and humiliation. No. Our reaction is to carry on as before and try and put the blame elsewhere. We blame population growth. It is the fault of the poor—there are too many of them. This at once lets us out of doing anything about the problems except talk about them—and blame the Catholic Church and the Mullahs of Islam for not allowing their rules on birth control to be changed.

Actually statistics do not bear out the accusation that the increasing numbers of the world's poor are responsible for the problems we face today. If we look at the figures we can see at once the uncomfortable truth that we, the rich, are responsible. This is not to say that increasing numbers is not a problem that must be tackled in the fight against poverty, hunger and disease, but it is not the poor that are putting the pressure on the world's resources at the moment. It is the lifestyles of the rich.

Energy is needed for everything that is produced. Production is a process of converting raw materials into finished goods and the conversion process needs energy. Even food production in modern agriculture needs large quantities of energy in its production and processing. So the amount of energy we use as a nation is a helpful indicator in showing the amount of resources being consumed. The richest country in the world is the United States. It is also the most energy hungry country in the world, consuming more energy than China, although the US has a population of about one fifth of that of China. If population and resource use were directly related (as of course they should be in a just and equitable world) then we should expect China to use more energy than any other country in the world. In fact, the average citizen in China uses only one tenth of the energy consumed by the average American.

Every country in the world aims at economic growth. This means an increase in the use of their resources and energy. But China could double its population and double its energy consumption and still barely be on a par with the US.

This pattern is found throughout the world when one compares population and energy consumption of the rich and poor countries. It shows clearly that there is not enough to go round not because of the numbers of the poor but because of the lifestyles of the rich. While we continue to live wastefully and greedily we are condemning the poor to perpetual poverty. Even if their populations remained constant or even dropped, the basic fact of life for them is that we are depriving them of their share by the way we live.

The importance of facing this truth is to show us that the responsibility for changing the face of the world lies in our hands, in the changes we make in our lives. The poor remain poor; the world continues to be poisoned; coal, gas, oil and other necessities of life are used up—because of our demands for more. This is not to say that strenuous efforts may not need to be made to control population growth, but to do this without fully acknowledging the real nature of our responsibilities is merely escaping reality.

Note that the dishonest steward was praised for his astuteness, not his dishonesty. Is there also a clever way of getting out of our problems without too much cost and suffering to ourselves? Jesus seems to be saying that although it is not God's way to help others because it is to our advantage, it is possible to improve our situation if we link our fate with the less fortunate and act in both our interests. The children of light, less worldly-wise, would never think of their own skins but only of those who needed their help. They would put their faith in God to provide for them, and help others out of love. We must not delude ourselves that our caring and sharing is a manifestation of our love for God if, in fact, we are just trying to save ourselves. We 'cannot be a slave of both God and money'.

Prayer
Most merciful Father, forgive me. My ways have not been your ways.

Action
Do you or your family use anything battery powered?— walkman, toys, torches? If batteries are essential buy a battery re-charger and some re-chargeable batteries. Batteries use up to 50 times more energy in their manufacture than they give. They contain dangerous metals such as cadmium and mercury and are therefore a health hazard on disposal. Avoid them wherever possible.

◆ *80% of the mercury emitted into the environment by French households comes from batteries.*
One third of the world's cadmium consumption goes into batteries.
World Watch Report, 1991

◆ *World oil consumption per person averages at 4.5 barrels a year.*
Average per person in the USA is 24 barrels a year.
Average per person in Western Europe is 12 barrels a year.
Average per person in sub-Saharan Africa is less than 1 per year.
World Watch Report, 1991

◆ *Estimates for oil production by 2030 are that it will be about half the output for 1990 because of reduction in oil reserves and environmental requirements.*
Given population increases this would allow an average of 1.2 barrels per person.
World Watch Report, 1991

Reading: *Job 38:2–7*

Who is this obscuring my designs with his empty-headed words? Brace yourself like a fighter; now it is my turn to ask questions and yours to inform me. Where were you when I laid the earth's foundations? Tell me, since you are so well-informed? Who decided the dimensions of it, do you know? Or who stretched the measuring line across it? What supports its pillars at their bases? Who laid its cornerstone when all the stars of the morning were singing with joy, and the Sons of God in chorus were chanting praise?

Today's reading begins with a dramatically challenging question from God. 'Who is this obscuring my designs?'

What is immediately striking in God's question is that it is precisely where we think our strength lies that God sees our greatest weakness and the cause of the failure of mankind to live according to God's will. It is our belief in our cleverness. 'Tell me, since you are so well-informed . . .' If you read the rest of this majestic passage (chapters 38 and 39), you will see that again and again God challenges us on our belief and confidence in our extensive knowledge and understanding of the mysteries and marvels of creation. It is painfully obvious that our knowledge, immense though it may seem, is in fact mean and paltry—because it fails to capture the majesty and wonder of creation. We are obsessed with reducing everything to its smallest explainable components, to a mechanical view of the universe, and so we miss seeing the wholeness and holiness of it all and finding our proper place in it.

Today God's words might have a similar thunderous challenge. How is it, since you are so clever and can reach the moon, that you cannot overcome the difficulties that prevent you feeding the hungry who are so near to you? How is it, since you claim to understand the workings of nature, that you cannot harness the wind, the waves and the sun for your power, but have to resort to methods which pollute and poison the earth? How is it, since you claim to understand the workings of human nature, that you cannot devise ways to live in peace except by possessing the threat of mutual extinction? How is it, since you claim to understand so much about man's economic life, that you cannot live in a way so that mankind can work to glorify his Creator and enjoy the fruits and blessings of the earth? How is it, since you claim to know so much about the workings of nature, that you are overburdening its inbuilt systems for cleansing and renewal so that many forms of life are threatened and natural mechanisms are breaking down? How is it that since you have replaced the law of God with your own wisdom, you have turned the world into a place where people are driven by fear and greed, where the air they breathe is increasingly poisoned, where the first invitation of God to man—to go and multiply—has become the curse on which the evils of the world are blamed?

These are indeed challenging questions to all of us who profess to follow the way of Christ. Can we brace ourselves like fighters and answer, or should we say like Job,

> *My words have been frivolous: what can I reply? I had better lay my finger on my lips. I have spoken once . . . I will not speak again; more than once . . . I will add nothing.*
> **(Job 39:34, 35)**

In such humble silence we can begin to listen to what God is telling us through his prophets, through the signs in his creation, and begin to understand the nature of the sin that is obscuring God's design.

Prayer

I know that you are all powerful: what you conceive, you can perform. I am the man who obscured your designs with my empty-headed words. I have been holding forth on matters I cannot understand, on marvels beyond me and my knowledge . . . I knew you then only by hearsay; But now, having seen you with my own eyes, I retract all I have said, and in dust and ashes I repent.
(Job 42:2, 3, 5, 6)

Action

Reconsider your balance sheet. Can you make any adjustments?

◆ *Plutonium has a half life of 24,000 years.*

◆ *Even if all nuclear arsenals were abolished tomorrow their waste products would remain.*

◆ *The United States military generates more hazardous waste than the total generated by the five largest US chemical companies. This does not include nuclear waste.* (State of the World 1991)

50

Note to group leader: The aim of these questions is to bring out an awareness of personal responsibility for the effect of our lifestyle on God's creation. If the discussions get stuck on the responsibilities of governments and transnational companies, ask the group to consider who buys the products from the transnationals and why people vote for the governments in question, etc. If the group is large enough divide into groups of two and three for the discussion and then share your answers and insights.

Useful props
1. Pencils and paper.
2. Objects damaging to the environment, e.g. aerosols, detergents, plastic bags, packaging, pesticides or weedkillers used in the garden, etc.
3. A table with a candle, matches and space for the objects to be placed.

Questions for discussion
1. What environmental damage distresses you most?
2. Who or what has caused it?
3. Why? Who benefits?
4. What would you do if you had political power?
5. What would you do if you had God's power?
6. What implications do your answers to 4 and 5 have on your life?

Preparation for worship
1. Using the objects provided as a stimulus, prepare prayers which express sorrow at our personal part in the destruction of God's creation.
2. Discuss how material that has emerged from the discussion could be incorporated into your worship.

Suggestions for worship

◇ **Begin with Psalm 51 [50].**

◇ **Mourning and lamentation (choose four readers):**

1. O God, I am in mourning for my river. Its water is foul smelling and full of slimy algae. The flowers I used to pick as a child have gone. Not a frog croaks. The fish are diseased.

2. O God, I was horrified by what happened at Chernobyl and how it affected countries as far away as ours. I dread what might happen here

51

with our nuclear industry and the disposal of nuclear waste, with polluted air and contaminated water causing disease and even death.

3. O God, I am weeping for the woods of Europe. They are dying and the dry branches accuse us because we have poisoned the ground. They can no longer breathe the air.

4. With a feeling of despair, I watch creation being destroyed. Animals and plants have been exterminated and are gone for ever. I see the uprooted trees, the ravaged mountains, the radioactive soil, the earth sealed in concrete.

ALL: LORD HAVE MERCY UPON US

from *Women's World Day of Prayer*, March 1992

◇ Pray together Job's prayer (in Week 2: Day 7).

◇ Individual prayers of sorrow and repentance. Bring the symbols and lay them on the table with each prayer.

◇ Read Isaiah 54:4–10.

3 *Repentance and Change*

Week 3: Day 1	Repentance

Reading: Joel 2:12, 13, 21, 22

But now, now—it is Yahweh who speaks— come back to me with all your heart, fasting, weeping, mourning. Let your hearts be broken, not your garments torn, turn to Yahweh your God again, for he is all tenderness and compassion, slow to anger, rich in graciousness, and ready to relent ... O soil, do not be afraid; be glad, rejoice, for Yahweh has done great things. Beasts of the field, do not be afraid; the pastures on the heath are green again, the trees bear fruit, vine and fig tree yield abundantly.

Joel is a wonderful book for all who recognize the failure of mankind to live out God's plan. The scenes of devastation he describes are as horrible as any predictions that environmentalists today make about the future of our world. 'Seeds shrivel under their clods ... the granaries lie in ruins, for lack of harvest ... The herds of cattle wander bewildered because they have no pasture ... Even the wild beasts wait anxiously for you, for the watercourses have run dry' (Joel 1:17–20). This is the fate of a people who have turned their backs on God. But Joel, a true prophet of God, has words of hope to give to all who truly repent and seek to change their ways. God does not want his people to suffer and longs for their return to him.

Today we learn what repentance means. It is not tearing our clothes because we fear the future and fear doing without. It is a deep inner sorrow—a broken heart—that what we have done has separated us from God. Repentance is a recognition that what is occurring is the fruit of our sin—yours and mine. It is the result of a failure to take seriously our common vocation as stewards and custodians of God's earth, and of treating it as our own. It is a failure to recognize that stewardship involves not only ourselves but the rest of mankind, all of whom have a share in this vocation but whom we are robbing of their chance to serve God by our selfishness and greed.

For many people, living ordinary, blameless lives, it is difficult to respond to God's call to repentance because it is hard to recognize what our sins are and, therefore, to feel that true deep sorrow and desire for change. Today we are called to recognize that sin has pervaded all our actions, that our very lifestyle is an act of rebellion against God's love. We can no longer look at sin as a private matter between ourselves and God, and blame the evils of the world on governments, industry, the feckless poor and the countless other scapegoats we have been accustomed to hold responsible. It is a matter for each one of us to respond to and to recognize our responsibility as individuals and as members of one another.

Last week we tried to face the fruit of our sin. This week, in our act of repentance, we will look at the roots of our sins so that we may understand how it is that we have unwittingly allowed ourselves to be taken captive so firmly by the enemy of God. For those who still believe that the problem is primarily an economic one and not the results of sin, the words of an economist, E. F. Schumacher, will perhaps give that broader perspective: 'The problem posed by environmental deterioration is not primarily a technical problem: if it were it would not have arisen in its acutest form in the technologically most advanced societies. It does not stem from scientific or technical incompetence, or from insufficient scientific education, or from lack of information, or from any shortage of trained manpower, or lack of money for research. It stems from the lifestyle of the modern world, which in turn arises from its most basic beliefs—its metaphysics, if you like, or its religion' (*Modern Pressures and the Environment*).

When we understand this then we have begun to walk the path to repentance, turning back to God, who will forgive us and renew our broken hearts so that we can truly rejoice in his promise: ' "I will make up to you for the years devoured by grown locust and hopper, by shearer and young locust, my great army which I sent to invade you." You will eat to your heart's content, will eat your fill, and praise the name of Yahweh your God who has treated you so wonderfully' (Joel 2:25, 26).

Prayer

Have mercy on me, O God, in your goodness, in your great tenderness wipe

away my faults; wash me clean of my guilt, purify me from my sin.
For I am well aware of my faults, I have my sin constantly in mind, having
sinned against none other than you, having done what you regard as
wrong.
(Psalm 51:1–4)

Action

Today's reading refers to the soil rejoicing. Buy organic vegetables and
fruit whenever possible, not only for your health, but for the sake of the
soil.

◆ *We Christians . . . are ourselves responsible for the misuse of the*
   resources God has given to the world. And our responsibility is not
   merely for other people but also for the political and economic
   structures that bring about poverty, injustice and violence. Today our
   responsibility has a new dimension because men now have the power
   to remove the causes of the evil, whose symptoms alone they could
   treat before . . . We do not despair in spite of the resistance of men and
   structure, with all their delays and frustrations, because we know that
   it is God's world, and that in Christ there is forgiveness and the chance
   to begin anew every day, step by step. God wants the world to develop,
   and He conquers and will conquer sin.
   WCC and Pontifical Justice and Peace Commission, Beirut

Week 3: Day 2   **The roots of sin**

Reading: *Genesis 3:1–7*

**The serpent was the most subtle of all the wild beasts that Yahweh
God had made. It asked the woman, 'Did God really say you were
not to eat from any of the trees in the garden?' The woman
answered the serpent, 'We may eat the fruit of the trees in the
garden. But of the fruit of the tree in the middle of the garden God
said, "You must not eat it, nor touch it, under pain of death." '
Then the serpent said to the woman, 'No! You will not die! God
knows in fact that on the day you eat it your eyes will be opened**

and you will be like gods, knowing good and evil.' The woman saw that the tree was good to eat and pleasing to the eye, and that it was desirable for the knowledge that it could give. So she took some of its fruit and ate it. She gave some also to her husband who was with her, and he ate it. Then the eyes of both of them were opened and they realized that they were naked. So they sewed fig-leaves together to make themselves loin-cloths.

In this simple story lies the root of our problems. It is a tragic story. The devil works so subtly that often we do not recognize that we have sinned. Just like a cancer that begins silently and secretly, so sin takes hold of us and, like cancer, often begins to show itself only when it is established and more difficult to root out. Because we have been unaware of its beginnings, we are baffled by its consequences.

The serpent's attack on Eve is subtle and clever.

First he questions her understanding of what God had really said: 'Did God really say that you were not to eat of any of the fruits of the garden?' Then he challenges her to think for herself and questions the whole validity of God's demands, suggesting that they are restrictions of her freedom. He gets at her through her feelings about herself, her self-esteem and her rights as a human being, which God's rules apparently deny. She has a right to be free: 'on the day you eat it your eyes will be opened.' She has a right to power: 'you will be like gods.' And she has a right to know and experience whatever she wants: 'knowing good and evil.'

All this seems to be part of being a thinking human being. We honour all these qualities in our society—freedom of thought and action, freedom to use the power with which we are invested, freedom to obtain all knowledge. Yet the story of the Fall seems to indicate that these things can be the cause of sin. The devil has succeeded by his subtle questioning and appeals to our feelings of self to direct our thought away from God towards our own desires. At that point we are open to sin and when he says that 'the day you eat it your eyes will be opened and you will be like gods', we cannot resist the temptation. Not content to be in the image of God, reflecting his goodness and love, we want to be God. But as soon as we turn away from God we are no longer able to reflect his glory. We become nothing—mirrors reflecting only darkness. But we still believe that we can be gods because we have gained knowledge and this gives us the illusion of greatness.

Today the tree of knowledge still stands in our midst and we do not know how to cope with it. Still God leaves us to make the choice of whether to reach out and eat or whether to say, 'No, there is more than enough for us already.' Is our ability to split the atom or harness nuclear power a manifestation of conquering the earth, or a desire to become 'like gods'? Are our advances in medical science, in particular birth technology, genetic engineering, and the vexed area of organ transplants, working with God or are we trying to become gods, creating and destroying at will? The secret of death is already ours. We have the power to destroy the whole of God's creation on earth. When we finally find the key to life, will we no longer need God? Will we have become gods?

Eve shared the fruit with Adam because she thought it looked good, tasted good, and she had been led to believe that it was going to benefit them. Her sin had the appearance of a kind, thoughtful gesture. She did not intend them both harm. The devil is very clever in making us believe that what we do will not affect others, that our lives are our affair. But we were made as helpmates for each other; each encounter with another human being produces a reaction for good or ill. We can reflect God and give another a glimpse of something wonderful, or we can reflect the darkness and lengthen the shadows over others.

Prayer
Lord Jesus Christ, Son of God, have mercy on me a sinner.

Action
Take your balance sheet. Use it for your prayer. Ask God's pardon for each item on the debit side and his help in changing it.

◆ *In Byelorussia 80,000 children still require specialized medical treatment as a result of the nuclear accident at Chernobyl in 1986.* **Greenpeace, 1991**

Week 3: Day 3	Other gods

| *Reading:* | Hosea 2:5, 8 |

'I am going to court my lovers,' she said 'who give me my bread and water, my wool, my flax, my oil and my drink...' She would not acknowledge, not she, that I was the one who was giving her the corn, the wine, the oil, and who freely gave her that silver and gold of which they have made Baals.

The book of Hosea begins with the tender imagery of the grief of the betrayed loving husband longing for the return of his faithless wife. She has failed to recognize that all she has comes from her husband and has turned to other lovers, mistakenly attributing all her material pleasures to them and to their hand-made gods.

Throughout the Old Testament we read of God's people turning away from God and putting their trust in false gods. Each time they are called back to repentance and we learn more about the longing of God to take his bride back into his arms, forgive her and restore her to her place in his affections. Sadly she generally fails to respond until her faithlessness turns against her and she realizes, with much suffering, her mistake.

This call to God always brings with it an emphasis on inner conversion. 'I desire not sacrifice. Circumcise your hearts.' 'I will take away this heart of stone and give you a heart of flesh.' The people's sin of apostasy was not always an obvious outer worship of false gods. Often an inner faithlessness was marked by an outward show of piety of the sort which Jesus condemned in the Pharisees when he said to them, 'You are the very ones who pass yourselves off as virtuous in people's sight, but God knows your hearts. For what is thought highly of by men is loathsome in the sight of God' (Luke 16:15).

It comes as a shock to us as Christians to be told that our hearts are focused on another god; that our real religion is other than Christianity. In these reflections we have tried to face a dimension in which we have failed—that the conservation of our world and the care of its creatures and resources is after all something that concerns us spiritually. Now we must take a further step and face the disconcerting truth that *the very way we think* is not that of a follower of Christ but that of a devotee of quite a different religion. The fate of the earth is now calling upon us to recognize this.

'It is here that the idea of conservation can be seen as the most necessary and at the same time as the most challenging of all ideas: it challenges the "sacred cow" of the modern world, namely the prevailing religion of economics which sees the primary meaning and purpose of human life in the limitless expansion of every man's needs, that is to say, his craving for more and more material satisfaction ... We cannot continue to deify economic progress in purely quantitative terms ... if it is not to lead to disaster it must be progress according to a new pattern, a pattern inspired by a profound understanding of, and a deep reverence for, our natural environment which is not man-made but God-given' (E. F. Schumacher, *The Economics of Conservation*).

St Paul makes this point too in his letter to the Colossians: 'That is why you must kill everything in you that belongs *only* to earthly life ... especially greed, which is the same thing as worshipping a false god; all this is the sort of behaviour that makes God angry. And it is the way in which you used to live when you were surrounded by people doing the same thing, but now you, of all people, must give all these things up' (Colossians 3:5–8).

Prayer
Thank you for your everlasting love which calls me back to you however far I have strayed.

Action
Read and reflect on Matthew 6:25–34. How far does verse 32 refer to you?

◆ *By the end of the century 10% of the world's population will hold 80% of the world's resources.*

◆ *Christians make up 32% of the world's population.*

◆ *Christians own 62% of the world's wealth.*

◆ *Christians spend 92% of it on themselves.*

◆ *Not all Christians are rich. Many live in extreme poverty in South and Central America, the Philippines and in Eastern Europe.*

Week 3: Day 4	The violence of today's religion

Reading: *Luke 16:16, 17*

'Up to the time of John it was the Law and the Prophets; since then, the kingdom of God has been preached, and by violence everyone is getting in. It is easier for heaven and earth to disappear than for one little stroke to drop out of the Law.'

John the Baptist preached repentance, and proclaimed that 'the kingdom of heaven is close at hand', and Jesus, in his teaching and his parables announced the good news that the Kingdom had come and is here. In his healing miracles he confirmed the words with which he opened his ministry, that slaves would be liberated, the deaf hear, the dumb speak, the lame leap for joy.

Yet in today's reading Jesus says some mysterious words which invite us to reflect on our whole concept of the kingdom of heaven on earth and our means to it. What can Jesus mean when he says, 'since then, the kingdom of God has been preached, and by violence everyone is getting in'?

It is tempting to look at the prosperous West, the Christian West, and come to the conclusion that our wealth is God's reward for our faith and a sign of the coming of the Kingdom on earth. If we look back over European history we see a close connection between Christianity, flowering culture and increasing wealth. Monasteries have been centres of culture and often great wealth, and missionaries have frequently been followed by traders and pioneers who have exploited the newly discovered resources of the nations being converted. We have liberated slaves, achieved remarkable cures for the sick, the halt and the lame, seen 'miracles' of increased productivity in agriculture and industry. Compared to other parts of the world the Christian West seems in many ways to have embodied heaven on earth.

If we examine how this has been achieved, it is less easy to make a Christian connection. It soon becomes apparent that we have built up our wealth by violent means and we are still doing so. When people work in factories, however beautiful and clean, and their work is monotonous, repetitive, boring, noisy and leaves no place for their own personalities to develop and their creativity to flourish, then it becomes soul- and mind-destroying and a form of violence against those people. Our heaven on earth is being gained by violence. The hope that such work will soon become unnecessary because it will be taken over by robots and computers, is just another form of violence, for the unemployment that results from such measures is replacing one form of violence by another. Unemployment robs people of their basic right and human need to work.

Our food is produced by violent means. Animals in factory farms are treated like machines; there is no thought for the distress caused by cramped conditions, restricted movement, a life in perpetual darkness to produce white meat, or perpetual light to produce more eggs. Crops depend on pesticides and herbicides—chemical warfare to destroy the 'enemies of production'—and fertilizers to force our crops to grow bigger and faster.

Husbandry, care, gentleness, love, kindness, the opposites of violence rarely find a place in our farms where farming methods pollute the water table on which all life depends, and innocent wildlife becomes a victim of disrupted habitats and food poisoned by chemicals.

Even our bodies do not receive tender care from us. We fill them with all sorts of rubbish and if they fall ill we do not stop to find out why they have become subject to the invading bacteria or virus so that we can adjust our lifestyles or the things we eat and drink accordingly. Nor do we take time to encourage the body, full of wonderful self-healing properties, to deal with the invading illness. We immediately apply drugs which, while sometimes destroying the infection, also have other violent effects on our bodies, sometimes barely noticeable and at other times very unpleasant.

Today's reading challenges us again to reflect on the disunity of the life we live today. This disunity is nothing new. It was present in the separation of religion and life by the Jews of Jesus' time. The Law, which was an outer expression of an inner spiritual reality, had become the reality. Instead of reflecting the consciousness of an ever-present God, the ritual of the Law had become the means to holiness.

Jesus is emphatic that he came to fulfil the Law and not destroy it. The Law is an expression of the holiness of everyday life and everyday actions—washing, cooking, working, praying. Jesus frees us from the tyranny of ritual and restores us to an awareness of God's presence in everything we do. If we accept the freedom he offers, we have to work even harder to maintain an inner awareness of God's presence in everything we do, while at the same time remembering that such an awareness is a blessing and a grace that only God can give to us. 'You must give up your old way of life; you must put aside your old self, which gets corrupted by following illusory desires. Your mind must be renewed by a spiritual revolution so that you can put on the new self that has been created in God's way, in the goodness and holiness of the truth' (Ephesians 4:22–24).

Today, when the disappearance of heaven and earth no longer seems such an impossibility, we can only reflect on the words of Jesus and the new law he gave us, which, he tells us, is more enduring than heaven and earth. He has given us the law of love, gentleness and peace. It is indivisible, all-embracing, and applicable to everything we do and to all creation.

If we ask why gentler, more loving methods are not used in modern life, the answer is always the same: 'It is uneconomic.' Our 'religion of economics' has blinded us to the message that Jesus came to preach and for which he died: that his love must permeate *every* corner of our lives, liberating us from other gods and religions. We have excluded our faith from many areas of our lives because it would be 'uneconomic', because 'religion should be kept out of politics', or 'because one has to be a realist'. We separate life and religion instead of letting our faith be the leaven in our lives that 'a woman took and mixed in with three measures of flour till it was leavened *all* through' (Matthew 13:33).

61

Prayer

Grandfather,
Look at our brokenness,
we know that in all creation
only the human family
has strayed from the sacred way.
We know we are the ones
who are divided.
And we are the ones
who must come back together
to walk in the sacred way.
Grandfather, Sacred one,
teach us love, compassion and honour
that we may heal the earth
and heal each other.
From the Ojibway nation of Canada

Action

If you have a garden, however small, start a compost heap. If you live in a flat with a balcony, start a worm bin for all your waste food stuffs and organic matter. Then grow herbs in pots with the resulting soil.

◆ *99% of all Britain's vegetables and cereals are sprayed with one or more pesticides.*

◆ *Over one tenth of all winter wheat in England and Wales is treated with nine or more chemicals.*
  Lloyd Timberlake, *Only One Earth*

Week 3: Day 5   **Awareness**

Reading: *Matthew 6:22, 23*

'The lamp of the body is the eye. It follows that if your eye is sound,

your whole body will be filled with light. But if your eye is diseased, your whole body will be all darkness. If then, the light inside you is darkness, what darkness that will be!'

Today's reading is another uncompromising statement about the all-embracing nature of our Christian beliefs. The 'eye' is either sound or diseased. There is no inbetween. The challenge to us is to recognize the disease in our outlook on life, to re- examine the way we live and the way we think, to see whether or not it accords in every way with the teaching of Jesus. This is very difficult when we are so used to separating 'religion' from 'life'. Much of what we thought had nothing to do with Jesus might now turn out to be the disease that is preventing us from seeing him clearly.

We have to go right back to basics. What is it that motivates us in our lives? Is it money, prestige, the good opinion of others? What do we believe are our rights? What do we think of the assumption that is fundamental to our Western way of life, that everything consumable should be allowed and accessible to everyone who wants it, and that the science and technology that make it all possible, should be given pride of place in our lives? For is it not our belief that only science and technology can, in the long run, bale us out of our problems?

The Word of God tells us repeatedly that false gods cannot save us. False religion, however meticulously followed, involving sacrifices (the poor and unemployed?), fasting (the monetarists?), studying sacred works (computer technology?), will not lead to enlightenment and the attainment of heaven.

> *For God says: 'I hate and despise your feasts, I take no pleasure in your*
> *solemn festivals. When you offer me holocausts, . . . I reject your*
> *oblations, and refuse to look at your sacrifices of fattened cattle. Let me*
> *have no more of the din of your chanting, no more of your strumming on*
> *harps. But let justice flow like water, and integrity like an unfailing*
> *stream.*
> **(Amos 5:21–24)**

We live in a limited world with limited resources and limited tolerance levels which the true God, the one God and Creator, has wisely put there to bring us back to him.

Once we recognize our false orientation we are faced with the question of what to do. How do we utterly destroy our false gods and follow the ways of truth and light? How can we replace our diseased eyes with a new, whole, pure vision?

First we must seek an awareness of what exactly it is we are worshipping. Each of us has our own private god—our aims and desires in life. We must take great care to identify them to recognize what it is upon which our security depends. John Dalrymple calls this a process of 'internalization of values'. 'We all have things we set our heart on, which determine our whole existence and "make us tick"... Jesus Christ had no time for this kind of living. He challenged his contemporaries to abandon these purely worldly and egocentric ambitions and see first the Kingdom of Heaven... Jesus expects us to be quite ruthless in this first step of jettisoning our possessiveness and becoming poor in spirit. He indulged in no condemnation of material things as such. (They are good, created by God.) But he launched into a strict condemnation of rich people who set their hearts on them and so did not have time or energy for spiritual things. The first growth point, then, in the Christian life is when we realize that material possessions are good things in themselves but must be spiritually surrendered in order that we may set our hearts on deeper things' (*Longest Journey*).

Honestly to surrender our possessions spiritually is very difficult and we will come back to this again later. Most of us need to do quite a bit of physical surrendering as well to learn to trust Jesus and abandon ourselves completely to his mercy. We know that he has assured us that 'all these other things will be given' if we set our hearts 'on his kingdom first, and on his righteousness' (Matthew 6:33), so we try to persuade ourselves that as we have turned our eyes towards Jesus we can carry on as before.

It is only when our eyes are truly focused on the Kingdom of God and we tread the path he ordains that these 'other things' find their rightful place in our lives. We are not asked to despise the material benefits of this world; they are there for us to enjoy and use in the service of God. If we use them only for our own ends it will lead to spiritual death and, as we are seeing in the world around us, physical destruction and death of the very things which we desire.

'See, today I set before you life and prosperity, death and disaster. If you obey the commandments of Yahweh your God, if you love Yahweh your God and follow his ways... you will live and increase... But if your heart strays, if you refuse to listen, if you let yourself be drawn into worshipping other gods and serving them, I tell you today, you will most certainly perish' (Deuteronomy 30:15–18).

Prayer

Yahweh, make your ways known to me, teach me your paths. Set me in the way of your truth, and teach me, for you are the God who saves me.
(Psalm 25:4, 5)

Action

Reflect on how you spend your time. How much is spent acquiring and maintaining your possessions. Does this reflect your priorities? Consult your balance sheet and pray about the debit side after adjusting it.

◆ *A typical resident of the industrialized nations consumes*
  15 times as much paper
  10 times as much steel
  12 times as much fuel, as a Third World resident.

◆ *This discrepancy is considerably higher in the USA.*
  World Watch Report, 1991

◆ *In Britain enough aluminium cans are thrown away each year that,*
  put end to end, they would reach to the moon and back.

◆ *In the USA aluminium waste could make 6,000 DC10 aircraft.*
  World Watch Report, 1991

Week 3: Day 6   Freedom from encumbrances

Reading: 1 Peter 1:13–16

Free your minds, then, of encumbrances; control them, and put your trust in nothing but the grace that will be given you when Jesus Christ is revealed. Do not behave in the way you liked to do before you learnt the truth; make a habit of obedience: be holy in all you do, since it is the Holy One who has called you, and scripture says: 'Be holy, for I am holy.'

'Encumbrances' can be many things beside material possessions. In his book *Holiness*, Donald Nicholl gives a very useful exercise in learning how to take this very first step in making our choice to abandon other gods and follow the road that leads first to Bethlehem and then to Calvary. The aim of this exercise is to free our minds from the encumbrances of possessions, of material and other burdens, so that Jesus can take his rightful place in our hearts. This exercise helps us to get a proper perspective on the engulfing material accumulation which surrounds us.

'Once we realize that we own absolutely nothing, we are enlightened, not only in the sense that our minds are flooded with light but also in the sense that a weight is lifted from us and our hearts grow lighter. Which is not to say, of course, that we immediately become *fully* enlightened; but at least we have made a true beginning when we can gaze around at all the possessions, qualities and capacities that are supposed to be ours and recognize that they do not really belong to us. In fact a good exercise for us as beginners is to scan slowly over the world we have built around us and say of every item in it, "Not mine; just on temporary loan": "This house—not mine, just on temporary loan; those books—not mine, just on temporary loan; these fingers—not mine, just on temporary loan; my mind—not mine, just on temporary loan." It takes a long time to carry out this exercise properly but when it is done properly the result is a clear mind and a light heart' (*Holiness*).

There are other results too: gratitude and awe at the immense confidence God must have in us to trust us with so much. When we realize this, then we cannot but respond with an attitude of responsibility and care towards those things. Our riches have all been lent to us. We are not at liberty to neglect them or destroy them at will. In this new freedom we can also understand more easily how it is possible to be detached without turning this detachment into a contempt or dismissal of the material and other goods we have at our disposal. God means us to live joyfully; he wants us to use and appreciate the good things of the world. He has not given us a sense of beauty, an enjoyment of food and wine, an ear for music, in order to tempt and test us. Nowhere are we given to believe that it is wrong to take pleasure in these things. But, as St Peter points out in our reading, we must not put our trust in them, or regard them as the purpose of our lives. Our freedom from such a dependence is a mark of our conversion. Since we 'have learnt the truth' we know that all we need, and all we can depend on, is the grace that Jesus Christ gives us.

'There is no need to worry; but if there is anything you need, pray for it, asking God for it with prayer and thanksgiving, and that peace of God, which is so much greater than we can understand, will guard your hearts and your thoughts, in Christ Jesus' (Philippians 4:6, 7).

Prayer

Lord, I thank you that you have trusted me with so many good things. Do not let me spoil your confidence by wanting to possess them for myself, but always lift my heart to you in joy and gratitude.

Action

Do Donald Nicholl's exercise in the room you are in now. Is there anything 'on loan' which you should now pass on to someone else because of their need for it? What have you finished with—books, clothes, household goods...?

◆ Road traffic contributes 84% of carbon monoxide, 50% of reactive hydrocarbons and 39% of nitrogen oxides released into the atmosphere by man.

◆ Passenger cars account for more than 13% of carbon dioxide, a major greenhouse gas causing global warming.

◆ 80% of cars are in the industrialized nations. Only 8% of humans own cars.

◆ In the UK
40% of households do not have a car.
70% of women do not hold a driving licence.

Week 3: Day 7   Seek your help from the Lord

Reading: *Isaiah 31:1–3*

Woe to those who go down to Egypt to seek help there, who build their hopes on cavalry, who rely on the number of chariots and on the strength of mounted men, but never look to the Holy One of Israel nor consult Yahweh.
Yet he too is skilled in working disaster, and he has not gone back on his word; he will rise against the house of the wicked, and against the protectors of evil men.
The Egyptian is a man, not a god, his horses are flesh, not spirit; Yahweh will stretch out his hand to make the protector stumble; the protected will fall and all will perish together.

The environmental problems we face today are so many and varied that there is room for different groups to be active in all sorts of ways. Some concentrate on pollution, others concentrate on wildlife, others work to alleviate poverty and famine. All are however united on one point: that the greatest threat to the world we live in, the environment we are trying to protect, is the threat of nuclear war.

Nuclear war would mean that 'all will perish together'. This is not to say that these groups are all agreed on what to do about nuclear weapons. The debate on whether disarmament or deterrent is the answer still goes on. It also goes on within the various churches, amongst the clergy and amongst the laity. Both sides use the Bible to justify their point of view. In between are many who do not know what to think, whose ability and willingness to think about the problem are limited by their fear of an unknown enemy and the unimaginable horror of a possible final war.

In trying to decide where we stand on this most crucial of all human questions we have to look at ourselves with a degree of honesty that perhaps no other question demands. This question goes right to the heart of everything we think we believe and everything we actually believe. I wonder whether this is why the churches have failed to come to a commonly held line, because the Holy Spirit is telling each one of us to look at ourselves to decide these questions?

Throughout the Old Testament, Egypt symbolizes slavery in return for material benefits. The children of Israel had food and shelter although they were enslaved and oppressed by the Egyptians. Often in the wilderness, when they found the insecurity of their freedom too hard to bear, they would cry out for the old days when they were enslaved but at least they 'were able to sit down to pans of meat and could eat bread' to their heart's content (Exodus 16:3). They had to be reminded constantly of the strength and power of God if only they would keep their sights on him instead of being distracted by material desires.

Is there not a connection between our reliance on 'weapons for peace' today and the children of Israel's cry against God? When we talk about protecting our freedom and way of life—what do we mean? Is it freedom to worship or freedom to be as rich as we can?

And who is paying for our freedom? We blame foreign governments for mismanagement of their funds while we pride ourselves on earning money by selling them arms; money which should go to help their people build up a viable agricultural and industrial base. We pat ourselves on the back for the 'aid' money we give, while demanding such high-interest payments on loans to the Third World debtor countries that they have to use their resources to pay us rather than feed themselves. The USA spends almost exactly the same amount on arms as it receives in interest payments from poor countries. Who is paying for the US military build up? It looks like the poor.

Today's reading invites us to dwell on some of these issues. Do we consider this a question for God or for us to decide? Is our religion part of our life, part of our politics? When we hear ourselves saying, 'It's all very well, but this is a matter of common sense, of life or death, not a matter for religion', then it is time to stop and ask ourselves what we mean by religion, what we think God's relevance to the world actually is.

Prayer
Lord, help me to have the courage to face my fears and discover the weakness of my faith in you and my enslavement to the ways of mankind.

Action
Write a letter to your MP about the issue you feel is most life threatening. Check with the address list at the back for the organizations which can help brief you on the facts and on how to write your letter.

Week 3:   Group discussion and worship—
                 Repentance and change

Note to group leaders: The aim of these questions is to bring an awareness of
the priorities and motivations that run our lives and to seek areas of change.

Useful props
1. Pencils and paper.
2. Small candles for each person.
3. Larger candle and matches.

Questions for discussion
1. What is the purpose of the main activity of your day?
2. What, if anything, would you prefer to do?
3. If you had five minutes to leave your house for ever what would you take with
you? What would you miss most about what you left behind?
4. It has been said that to live simply you either have to be very rich or have a
great deal of time. Do you agree? What do you think are the attributes necessary
to live simply?
5. Are 'standards' compatible with simplicity?
6. Discuss 'Action' so far. Share your successes and failures. Share your own
ideas.

Preparation for worship
1. Invite each person to prepare a prayer of repentance for their false gods/false
priorities/false motivations.
2. Invite each person to prepare a prayer of commitment to change, asking
God's help and guidance.

Suggestions for worship

◇ **Darken the room as much as possible, leaving only the central
   candle.**

◇ **Pray Psalm 32 [31].**

◇ **All light candles from the central candle and pray together:**

**Lord, you created the world in perfection and gave it to us in love. Your
light is our light.**

◇ **Each person prays their prayer of repentance and blows out
   their candle.**

◇ All pray together: Lord, you created the world in perfection and gave it to us in love. Forgive us for our unfaithfulness which has plunged the world into the darkness of sin. Send us again the light of your Spirit of Wisdom to overcome the darkness.

◇ Read John 1:4, 5, 9

All that came to be had life in him and that life was the light of men, a light that shines in the dark, a light that darkness could not overpower. The Word was the true light that enlightens all men; and he was coming into the world.

◇ Read John 8:12

When Jesus spoke to the people again, he said: I am the light of the world; anyone who follows me will not be walking in the dark; he will have the light of life.

◇ Each pray their prayer of commitment as they re-light their candle.

◇ All say together: You, Jesus, are the light of the world. If we follow you we will no longer walk in the darkness of sin, but will have the light of life. Alleluia.

4 *God Works Through Us*

Week 4: Day 1   **I count**

Reading: Isaiah 49:1–5

Islands, listen to me, pay attention, remotest peoples. Yahweh called me before I was born, from my mother's womb he pronounced my name.

He made my mouth a sharp sword, and hid me in the shadow of his hand. He made me into a sharpened arrow, and concealed me in his quiver.

He said to me, 'You are my servant (Israel) in whom I shall be glorified'; while I was thinking, 'I have toiled in vain, I have exhausted myself for nothing';

and all the while my cause was with Yahweh, my reward with my God. I was honoured in the eyes of Yahweh, my God was my strength.

What a marvellously encouraging passage. In the face of the huge global problems nothing is more tempting than to give up. How can anything I do possibly affect the world? Peace, a cleaner environment, the alleviation of poverty, the reduction of suffering in its many forms—these seem to be matters for governments, not individuals. This feeling becomes so strong that some give up, others become desperate and turn to violence, trying to bring a change in

72

'the system', the powers which are held responsible for the evil in the world. We must constantly remind ourselves that we are part of that system by the way in which we live. Structural injustice exists because of our demands, with our assent, because of our failure to stand up and witness to God's law.

We have acknowledged our responsibility and today we see the other side of the coin. I may be responsible but I am also indispensable in the solution of the problems I have helped to bring about. My responsibility goes out to the 'remotest peoples' because God has chosen me especially. For this I was born. Later in this chapter of Isaiah (verse 16) God says, 'See, I have branded you on the palm of my hands.' Not only are we chosen to play our part in his plan but he carries us with him always. Isaiah could hardly have put this point across more strongly, for once branded onto God's hands we are there always—either to show off beauty, like a ring adorning a perfect hand, or to disfigure him, like an ugly scar spoiling loveliness. We cannot be indifferent or neutral. By not playing our part we leave an unfillable gap. In human affairs we are dispensable; in the affairs of God there is no one but us to do our work.

The Bible consists of examples of people who understood and responded to this beautiful and awe-inspiring truth. Some, like Moses, were less willing at first. I find the debate between God and Moses a great consolation when I feel faced with a daunting task. (See Exodus 3 and 4:1–17.) Moses is full of self-doubt but God assures him that he will give Moses the powers when he needs them or that he will give him someone to help. Like Moses, we can put all our self-doubts before God and he will take them from us and give us the strength to do whatever he bids us. 'Yes, my yoke is easy and my burden light' (Matthew 11:30). Others, like Noah, Samuel, John the Baptist and the disciples came 'at once'. Mary, the mother of Jesus, responded most perfectly of all with her beautiful acceptance: 'I am the handmaid of the Lord, let what you have said be done to me' (Luke 1:38). Each of them let God take over and direct them in their designated task. They did not worry about all the other things that needed to be done as well, but left those to God.

We have examples about us today of people who have responded to their individual call and, not allowing themselves to be distracted by the many other problems about them, have singlemindedly and thoroughly carried out their tasks. Most of them are anonymous; some like Mother Teresa are well known to us. I am particularly moved by the example an old French shepherd gave. During the first world war, too old to fight for his country, this man spent his time looking after his sheep. But he was filled with the longing to do something for his country in its hour of need. Every day, as he minded his sheep, he collected acorns and planted them in the scrubland where he grazed his flock. Throughout the war years he planted thousands of trees and today there are acres of forest which give testimony to his act of faith. He, of course, never saw the fruits of his labours. He just did what he believed to be right while he could.

For some of us our first task will be to make reparations for what we see as our particular responsibility. Hammond Innes, the best-selling author, has recently given us a fine example of this. Realizing that countless trees had been used to make the paper on which the thousands of copies of his books are printed, he has been planting trees in an act of reparation and thanksgiving. This attitude should pervade all our activities. In it lies the possibility of a sustainable world.

Lest we should become daunted with the responsibility, Isaiah reminds us that God always gives us the wherewithal to do whatever he asks of us (verse 2). The sharp sword of speech, and the arrow hidden in the quiver remind us of the hidden power of God's word. They are lovely images of a strength emanating from a life rooted in God.

Prayer

Help us in this hour of crisis, the help that man can give is worthless. With God among us, we shall fight like heroes, he will triumph over our enemies. (Psalm 108:12, 13)

Action

We can't replace the fossil fuels we use for lighting, heating and cooking. Turn off all unnecessary appliances. Hang your washing outside. If you really need a dishwasher make sure you only use it when it is full.

Week 4: Day 2	God's instrument

Reading: *Romans 12:3–5*

In the light of the grace I have received I want to urge each one among you not to exaggerate his real importance. Each of you must judge himself soberly by the standard of the faith God has given him. Just as each of our bodies has several parts and each part has a separate function, so all of us, in union with Christ, form one body, and as parts of it we belong to each other.

Once we begin to respond to God's call we soon need the very important reminder in this passage. It brings us back to that central and much misunderstood part of Christian living: humility. Once we are aware of our uniqueness and importance in God's eyes, it is very tempting to start looking for results in everything we do. We think we are called to save the world singlehanded. Why, after all, we argue, should God ask me to do something that is not obviously successful? Is success not a sign of his calling? But God's ways are not our ways. Success can lead to pride, failure to a feeling that perhaps we have got it wrong or that God has not seen the importance of what we are doing after all. Today he reminds us that our uniqueness is like the uniqueness of an organ in the human body. The body cannot function without it but it is useless without the body it serves. Our task is not to take over the body but to work quietly and humbly so that the whole can be a healthy, well-functioning organism. A noisy, rumbling stomach calls attention to itself but that does not help it perform its function; a palpitating heart or fidgeting hands and feet serve no purpose except to distract.

The humble image of the body is particularly useful when we remember that we form it 'in union with Christ', with Christ as head, guiding and directing us. We are concerned simply with doing what we are told and not with the results of what we do. 'Work for the Lord with untiring effort and with great earnestness of spirit. If you have hope, this will make you cheerful. Do not give up if trials come; and keep on praying' (Romans 12:11, 12).

The individual success we crave for has no place in a team. We are in God's hands, subject to his timing. We work not for success but because we must do what we believe to be right. E. F. Schumacher puts it quite simply: 'We must do what we conceive to be the right thing, and not bother our heads or burden our souls with whether we are going to be successful. Because if we don't do the right thing, we'll be doing the wrong thing and we will just be part of the disease and not part of the cure.'

A wonderful example of this attitude is St Peter Chanel, the Marist saint who was martyred in the South Sea Islands last century. He preached the gospel tirelessly for years without any visible success. When the islanders finally turned on him and murdered him he had made fewer than a dozen converts. Yet his presence among them had had its effect and within a few years the entire island turned to Christianity. St Peter Chanel remained faithful to death, despite his apparent failure. In God's time his work bore fruit.

St Ignatius Loyola said, 'Act as if everything depended on you, and pray as if everything depended on God.' And St Teresa of Avila reminds us:

Christ has no body now on earth but yours.
Yours are the only hands with which he can do his work.
Yours are the only feet with which he can go about the world.
Yours are the only eyes through which his compassion can shine forth
upon a troubled world.
Christ has no body now on earth but yours.

75

Prayer

Use me then, Lord, for whatever purpose, and in whatever way you may require. Here is my poor heart, an empty vessel; fill it with your grace. Here is my sinful and troubled soul; quicken it and refresh it with your love. Take my heart for your abode; my mouth to spread abroad the glory of your name; my love and all my powers, for the advancement of your believing peoples; and never suffer the steadfastness and confidence of my faith to abate, so that at all times I am enabled from the heart to say, 'Jesus needs me, and I am his.'

(Dwight L. Moody)

Action

Reflect on the work you believe that God wants you to do. Do you tailor your lifestyle to this task? Try to identify what hinders you and wastes your time or distracts you.

Week 4: Day 3	Start from where you are

Reading   *Luke 3:10–14*

When all the people asked him, 'What must we do, then?' he answered, 'If anyone has two tunics he must share with the man who has none, and the one with something to eat must do the same.' There were tax collectors too who came for baptism, and these said to him, 'Master, what must we do?' He said to them, 'Exact no more than your rate.' Some soldiers asked him in their turn, 'What about us? What must we do?' He said to them, 'No intimidation! No extortion! Be content with your pay!'

'What must we do, then?' This question comes from the depths of our hearts. If only someone like John the Baptist would come and tell us what to do. 'Office workers—do this; housewives—do that; civil servants—act this way; government officials—enact those laws; labourers—behave this way; factory workers—approach your tasks that way; unemployed— fill your time with this; elderly and sick—cope with your sufferings like that.' The list would be endless. But it reminds us of an important point contained in this passage, where John the Baptist is appearing to fill this need. Although he gives some general rules for life, such as sharing and caring for those less fortunate than ourselves, and we can also take his words to each group of enquirers to hold truths for all of us: honesty in all we do, fairness, non-violence—he is also showing us in his different answers to different people that each of us must *start from where we are*. Neither soldiers nor tax collectors were regarded as the sort of people who could take the word of God seriously. Their jobs made them sinners. Yet they were not told to stop what they were doing but to change their lives from within that framework.

This message comes through repeatedly in the gospels. Different people ask Jesus, 'What shall we do to be saved?' His answers always go straight to the heart of the matter *for that individual*. Each one has particular attachments to overcome before Jesus can enter their lives. The rich young man had to overcome the domination of wealth, another disciple the call of his family. How hard-hearted Jesus must have seemed when he said, 'Leave the dead to bury their dead' (Matthew 8:22)—but how strong that image is! Our yearning for what is past and gone can so often prevent us from living in the present where God is to be found.

This means that we do not waste time dreaming of being St Francis or Gandhi, but that we look at ourselves in the situation we are in. Even the most insignificant adjustments to our lives can make a huge difference if enough of us undertake them. It has been calculated that if the most efficient light bulbs available today were used by the Americans, they would save one third of their coal-fired electricity. Even more staggering is the thought that if the Americans used more efficient cars, raising fuel economy to 40 miles per gallon, they would save as much energy as Brazil now consumes annually.

We are bound to ask: Why does this not happen? What stops governments acting? But perhaps we should be asking—why do I not act? Switching off lights and turning off taps seems insignificant, saving newspapers and empty bottles for recycling is just a drop in the ocean, but if we can do it, it is a beginning. Each one of us will have a different idea to begin with and once we have taken that first step towards adjusting our lifestyles we will discover that it is possible to change our attitude towards resources and the created world. Mother Teresa, faced with the enormity of the poverty and deprivation in India, does not spend her time travelling the world telling governments what to do. Quietly and lovingly she stoops and picks up the sick and dying, valuing each individual life and encountering Jesus in each sad and suffering face. 'We ourselves feel that what we are doing is just a drop in the ocean,' she says. 'But if that drop was not in the ocean, I think the ocean would be less because of that missing drop. I do not agree with the big way of doing things. To us what matters is an individual' (*A Gift for God*).

Prayer

I contemplate your coming, Lord, small and helpless, a baby in the manger. Let me remember that small and humble beginnings are not to be dismissed as useless, for they may contain within them the possibilities of changing the face of the earth.

Action

Resolve to buy an energy-efficient light bulb for your most used light next time you go shopping.

◆ *Although 94% of consumers believe in recycling, only 41% of those regularly take bottles, cans or newspapers to a collection point.*
The Independent, **21.1.92**

◆ *UK government target is 25% of household waste to be recycled by AD2000.*

◆ *1992 rate is 5%.*

◆ *One step at a time is enough for me.*
Gandhi

Week 4: Day 4   **Pray without ceasing**

Reading: *Ephesians 1:9–12*

He has let us know the mystery of his purpose, the hidden plan he so kindly made in Christ from the beginning to act upon when the times had run their course to the end: that he would bring everything together under Christ, as head, everything in the heavens and everything on earth. And it is in him that we were claimed as God's own, chosen from the beginning, under the predetermined plan of the one who guides all things as he decides

by his own will; chosen to be, for his greater glory, the people who would put their hopes in Christ before he came.

When we spend time with God in prayer we try to lift ourselves above the humdrum of everyday life and focus our minds on heavenly things, as if ordinary life was not suitable for God's ears. It is so hard to bring Jesus down into our everyday lives, to make the smallest action a celebration, an act of worship, and so fulfil God's plan in Jesus to bring together 'everything in the heavens and everything on earth'.

This unity in the minutiae of our daily lives is what distinguishes us from those who have not 'put their hopes in Christ', which sets us out as people chosen by God to fulfil his plan. The problem is that when we want to spend more time in prayer, when we want to follow some spiritual course, we find it is difficult to find the time. But when we see the unity in all things we can begin to overcome this problem.

I have found this a hard lesson to learn. As a mother of small children I have struggled for years feeling hampered by my inability to find space for prayer. It almost seemed as if God was trying to rob me of these precious moments of prayer and reflection. Each time I organized my life to make such spaces he seemed to send something else along to fill them. Advice like 'Offer up your tasks, that is prayer' seemed to imply to me an attitude of suffering and resignation about my daily chores which I did not feel or believe was right. At last it dawned upon me that perhaps God was trying to show me the unity in everything, that even prayer is not something to be separated from 'real' life.

How perfectly he teaches us this in the prayer he gave us. The Lord's Prayer is our model of how to pray. Its words reach up to heaven while, at the same time, they remain firmly rooted in the dreary details of everyday life. 'Our Father in heaven . . . give us this day our daily bread.' God is present in all we do and we can begin to pray without ceasing simply by becoming aware of his presence at all times. Then, not only does the washing up become a holy act because it is done in the presence of God, but one is filled with joy at the knowledge of such company. The remarkable thing that happens then is that suddenly one begins to become aware that there are spaces in the day where the noise and rush of life stop and God is there for a moment of more intense intimacy and communion. It often needs self-discipline to grab these moments, to stop and give them to God. But they become the most precious moments of the day when we do. 'Love to pray,' says Mother Teresa. 'Feel often during the day the need for prayer, and take trouble to pray. Prayer enlarges the heart until it is capable of containing God's gift of himself. Ask and seek, and your heart will grow big enough to receive him and keep him as your own' (*A Gift for God*).

The exercise of detaching ourselves from our possessions is extended into our spiritual life. My particular attachment at that time was what I regarded as my 'proper spiritual life'— certain times of the day for prayer, daily Mass. By being attached to this I was unable to see that daily tasks were also relevant to my relationship with God and that my narrow view of this relationship was preventing its growth.

This discovery brought a new freedom. While 'time for prayer' is still essential, prayer can pervade each moment of our lives if we recognize that even in the smallest decision God has something to say to us. In that part of our Christian vocation that concerns care of God's creation it is surprising how everyday decisions can lead to new opportunities to meet God. I found a new freedom in more senses than one when I realized that car exhausts damage the environment and decided to walk or bicycle wherever possible. What a joy to be able to experience a new contact with the world about me: bird song, smells of flowers and trees that surprise me in the grimmest, dirtiest part of town. I notice the seasons, I have a new opportunity to talk to my children as we walk each day to school. The joy and gratitude I feel becomes a prayer.

Our lives are made up of many insignificant examples like this, as we try to meet God in the smallest decisions we make in daily life. There is no laid down code of rules and regulations. Christ has freed us from that mentality. Each one of us has to make our own choice within the circumstances in which God has placed us. 'When Christ freed us, he meant us to remain free' (Galatians 5:1).

'Christ our Lord wanted us to learn the art of linking heaven and earth. He wanted to show how to harmonize heavenly and earthly things while awakening in us the same affinity for the heavenly as for the earthly, for the supernatural as for the natural. He wanted to teach us to behave like God on earth, and on God's earth to strive after heaven. For, after all, the redemption took place on earth and *"gratia supponit naturam"*—grace builds on nature ... It was Christ's intention to teach us that the kingdom of heavenly grace and the kingdom of our daily bread are on the same level ... Christ taught us through his wonderful gifts to see things concretely, that the man who was God must walk the earth, for we go over the earth to reach heaven' (Cardinal Stefan Wyszynski, *Our Father*).

Prayer

Lord, where shall I find you? Your place is hidden and high;
   Yet where shall I not find you? Your glory fills all space.
(*Service of the Heart*)

Action

Reflect again on how you spend your time. Do you find it hard to find enough time for prayer and Bible reading? What do you do that takes priority? Does it reflect your priorities? Pray about it.

Reading   *Luke 10:38–42*

In the course of their journey he came to a village, and a woman
named Martha welcomed him into her house. She had a sister
called Mary, who sat down at the Lord's feet and listened to him
speaking. Now Martha who was distracted with all the serving,
said, 'Lord, do you not care that my sister is leaving me to do the
serving all by myself? Please tell her to help me.' But the Lord
answered: 'Martha, Martha,' he said, 'you worry and fret about so
many things, and yet few are needed, indeed only one. It is Mary
who has chosen the better part; it is not to be taken from her.'

This story sums up our dilemma. We are torn between the Martha in us and the
desire to be like Mary, sitting at the feet of Jesus, listening, worshipping and
loving him in silence and peace. Martha is the active person in us. We see her as
the realist who recognizes that people need to be fed, that work has to be done to
keep the world going round, that even the Son of God needs food and shelter.

The dilemma is at its worst when we celebrate the great feasts of our faith at
Christmas and Easter. Celebration and togetherness mean work, for women
especially—shopping, preparing food, cleaning and tidying, buying presents.
Christmas particularly seems a burden, not just because it involves so much
work and expense but because the contrast of our spending with the poverty of
so much of the world makes our affluence at this time seem gross. Our pleasure
is marred by the knowledge that many millions have nothing.

Are such celebrations wrong? Should we give them up and, like Mary, spend
the time 'at the Lord's feet' and turn our backs on the presents and the food? Is
this the answer to the manifold crises in the world? Our savings would go to the
poor; there would certainly be less rubbish to engulf us. But what about our
friends and family? And what about the fact that at Christmas we are celebrating
the most wonderful gift to the world, the Christ Child, our salvation, the means
to eternal life, bread of life, living water? This gift calls for rejoicing and
celebration, the spreading and sharing of love.

So the dilemma persists and we can only turn to Jesus for an answer. What
guidance does he give us in his words to Martha? First of all, he points out to her
that she is 'distracted' by the work she is doing. This is a sure sign that we are out
of balance. We have to try and combine the care of Martha and the love of Mary.
'Distracted' means that the heart is engaged with things other than the
important. It has been said, 'If you are too busy to pray, you are too busy.'
But often it is the demands of others that take up our time and we feel that the

most loving thing to do is to give people the time they need. This happened to Jesus too. He was often unable to get away from the crowds for his own time for silence and prayer. On one occasion when he and the disciples tried to get away for some quiet, the crowd found out where they were going and followed him. 'So as he stepped ashore he saw a large crowd; and he took pity on them and healed their sick' (Matthew 14:14). After feeding the crowd (5,000 people), he sent the disciples away to rest while he said goodbye to the people. Again his concern was not for himself but for the others. He was not 'distracted' but quietly and calmly carried on his work until it was finished. At all times his heart was fixed on God; he was never distracted by the material demands that were put on him.

One of the reasons for becoming easily distracted by our work is that we have too many different tasks to do. 'You worry and fret about too many things, and yet few are needed, indeed only one.' This is the key to our dilemma. Simplicity in everything we do allows time for Jesus, time to listen without distraction, time to give to that one thing that matters.

Simplicity is the natural outcome of prayer and detachment. From the earliest days of Christianity it has been fundamental to Christian living. The crib at Christmas reminds us that Jesus was born in a stable, not a palace; his first companions were dumb animals and shepherds, simple folk, terrified of the extraordinary events they had witnessed on the hillside. But they responded at once and hurried off to see what had happened, not pausing to wash and change or make great preparations. At Easter the bare wood of the cross carrying the naked Christ reminds us that the Christian message has a stark simplicity, that love overcame sin.

Jesus' example of simplicity in his birth, his own lifestyle and his words, reminds us that it is a call given to every Christian. It is a call to which Christians have responded in different ways and to which the different traditions in the church bear witness. We need to study these different models which our history can show us, for in them lies the answer to many of the problems we face today. John XXIII wrote in his *Journal of a Soul*: 'The older I grow the more clearly I perceive the dignity and winning beauty of simplicity in thought, conduct and speech; a desire to simplify all that is complicated and to treat everything with the greatest naturalism and clarity.'

This is one of the marks of the saint and the mark of an eye trained only on Jesus, a heart filled only with him, a mind engaged on the only important matter there is: the will of God.

Prayer

Father, may your name be held holy in my life,
Your kingdom come in my heart,
Your will be done in me.

Action

If you feel tense with too many demands on your time today: STOP for five minutes. Sit down, with both feet squarely on the ground. Stay still, breathing calmly and steadily and ask God to take over.

Week 4: Day 6	The temple of the Holy Spirit

Reading: *1 Corinthians 6:19, 20*

Your body, you know, is the temple of the Holy Spirit, who is in you since you received him from God. You are not your own property; you have been bought and paid for. That is why you should use your body for the glory of God.

It is often said that our bodies are our property with which we can do as we please. We feel very protective towards our body; taking care over how it looks, making it comfortable and satisfying its demands. We are more inclined to protest at hazardous pollution if it affects the health of our bodies than if it damages the world around us. As evidence mounts that lead in car exhausts can cause brain damage in children, that the malformations in cattle and the higher-than-average incidence of leukaemia around the Sellafield nuclear processing plant is likely to be due to radioactive pollution in the area, that pollution from factory chimneys can cause lung disease, we are more inclined to protest and demand that the government 'do something'.

Yet while we blame others for the dangers to our health we often fail to take responsibility where it is ours to take. 'Your body, you know, is the temple of the Holy Spirit.' The food we eat and the care we take of our bodies are all part of the way in which we acknowledge God as our creator and worship him. 'Whatever you eat, whatever you drink, whatever you do at all, do it for the glory of God' (1 Corinthians 10:31).

This casts an interesting light on the many rules and regulations on food and cleanliness held by the Jews. They understood that their attitude towards their bodies was part and parcel of their relationship with God. What they ate, how they cared for their bodies, had a bearing on their inner lives. When Jesus taught the people that 'what goes into the mouth does not make a man unclean; it is what comes out of the mouth that makes him unclean . . .' (Matthew 15:10–20), he was not condemning the Law but was bringing them back to the truth that it is not external rituals that are important but the inner attitudes they reflect. He was not teaching that it does not matter what we do to our bodies or what we feed them with. As St Paul tells us, we are not our own property. We are stewards even of our body, which is God's property and must therefore be treated with respect and cared for so that we *can use it to further God's work on earth*. A person who loves God will not deliberately want to harm the body God has given him by pushing into it food likely to harm and hinder its effective use.

While what we eat does not in itself make us holy, it is relevant to our lives as people of God. Our Christian worship is centred around the eating of a meal. Human food—bread and wine—has a profound religious significance, bringing nourishment and healing to our souls. This was Jesus' last legacy to us and as everything in our religion is rooted in reality so we should meditate on this spiritual meal in relation to our earthly meals. The way we eat and what we eat does have spiritual significance. It is an important sign of togetherness and love to sit around a table together. The care we take in preparation of food is a sign of our care for those who share it with us. Yet we can use our celebrations as an opportunity to give thanks, worship and adore God, or we can show our disregard for God's property by our lavish excesses.

When God gave the Jews their laws on food he ended by saying, '...you have been sanctified and have become holy, because I am holy' (Leviticus 11:44). Jesus in the manger, Jesus at the marriage at Cana, Jesus feeding the five thousand, Jesus at the last supper, Jesus eating fish on the beach with his disciples after his resurrection, is visible proof of this sharing in the holiness of God in our human bodies.

Prayer
Bless this body you have given me. It is the temple of the Holy Spirit within me. Teach me to care for it because it is yours and forgive me for abusing it because I think it is mine.

Action
Think about your own meals with your family, your friends, or eaten on your own. Do you give thanks to God for his gifts? Has this become a ritual? Is this an opportunity to give thanks for more than just the food on the table? Try lighting a candle before you say grace as a focus and reminder that Christ, the light of the world, is present. Then ask for his blessing on your meal and all who are present.

◆ *'Before a man eats and drinks he has two hearts'* (The Talmud). *(He not only feels and thinks of his own hunger but also that of others. Once he has satiated his hunger and thirst he has only one heart, that which thinks only of his own needs and desires.)*

Week 4: Day 7   It is getting very late

Reading: *Mark 6:35–42*

By now it was getting very late, and his disciples came up to him and said, 'This is a lonely place and it is getting very late, so send them away, and they can go to the farms and villages round about, to buy themselves something to eat.' He replied, 'Give them something to eat yourselves.' They answered, 'Are we to go and spend two hundred denarii on bread for them to eat?' 'How many loaves have you?' he asked. 'Go and see.' And when they had found out they said, 'Five, and two fish.' Then he ordered them to get all the people together in groups on the green grass, and they sat down on the ground in squares of hundreds and fifties. Then he took the five loaves and the two fish, raised his eyes to heaven and said the blessing; then he broke the loaves and handed them to his disciples to distribute among the people. He also shared out the two fish among them all. They all ate as much as they wanted.

'By now it was getting very late.' These are the kinds of words one hears frequently from people who are monitoring the state of the world. 'Time is running out' they say. Reading the statistics confirms the feeling that many of the problems have become irreversible. We will need some kind of miracle if we are to save the earth for our children.

The most dangerous threats are those which cannot be conclusively proved and their source traced. No one wants to take on the responsibility. The sources of acid rain are one of these disputed menaces and so those responsible can evade taking action. Yet scientific studies in the 1980s show that 'reduced sulphur emissions are likely to bring direct environmental benefits although it may be 20–30 years before lakes and rivers can fully recover. Forest damage appears to start suddenly but is, in fact, preceded by a long period of "invisible damage" when growth slows down. Nobody knows if forests can recover' (*Friends of the Earth Bulletin*).

In today's reading Jesus does not comment on the lateness of the hour. It does not seem to concern him as it does the disciples. He spends no time wondering whether the people can find food elsewhere, how long it would take them, making calculations about how much food is needed, or the cost to himself or the disciples. All this would waste time. He gets straight down to work. 'Give them something to eat yourselves. How many loaves have you? Go and see.'

The lateness of the hour, the seriousness of the problem, the enormity of the task before us does require a miracle. But miracles do not take place if people sit around and wait for them to happen. They require faith and action. Our response to the crisis we face is based on our belief that God has a plan for the world and that we are part of that plan. With our co-operation he can accomplish miracles. There is no time to debate whether our particular contribution is worth making because too few others are responding with us. We dare not console ourselves with hopes that governments will act in time, thus allowing us to carry on as we were before until they do. There is only one possible answer to the question 'Can we save the world?' and that is 'Only if *I* play my part and if *I* begin now'.

The first thing Jesus told the disciples to do was to look at the resources they had available. This can be our first step too. We must find out what is happening, who is campaigning, and ask them how we can become involved. Once we join forces with others we become more effective. All the disciples worked together organizing the people, distributing the loaves and fish, and finally clearing up. It was an immense organizational task made possible by the presence of Jesus and their willingness to share the work.

Prayer

Let there be peace on earth
And let it begin with me.
Let there be love on earth
And let it begin in my heart.
Let there be miracles on earth
And let them begin with my faith.
Let there be a future
And let it begin with my actions—now.

Action

Find out about local groups and ask if you could publicize them on the notice board or in the church bulletin.

Note for group leader: The aim of the questions is to foster an awareness that each one of us is called by God to serve him in a particular way. Sometimes we are called out of our daily life, other times we remain within it.

Useful props
1. Pencils and paper
2. Sprig of flowering tree or shrub
3. Candle on a small table, matches

Questions for discussion
1. Who do you know whose life is spent serving God?
2. How do you spend your day? Work/leisure/voluntary work?
3. How is God asking you to serve him in your daily work?
4. Does your lifestyle serve your work for God or is it separate?

Preparation for worship
1. Write down on a piece of paper the way in which God has called you to serve him.
2. Prepare a prayer in which you tell God that you accept his calling and ask for his help and guidance.

Suggestions for worship

◇ Read Isaiah 49:1–6.

◇ Each offer their prayer of acceptance while laying their 'vocation' paper on the table by the lighted candle.

◇ Group leader holds up sprig of flowering tree or shrub and says to each member of the group in turn '(name) what do you see?' Each answers, 'I see a branch of the watchful tree.' When all have answered the group leader says: 'Well seen! God says "I too watch over my word to see it fulfilled."' (From Jeremiah 1:11, 12)

◇ Read:

'There is a variety of gifts but always the same Spirit; there are all sorts of service to be done, but always to the same Lord; working in all sorts of different ways in different people, it is the same God who is working in all of them. The particular way in which the Spirit is given to each person is for a good purpose' (1 Corinthians 12:4–7).

'People must think of us as Christ's servants, stewards entrusted with the mysteries of God. What is expected of stewards is that each one should be found worthy of his trust' (1 Corinthians 4:1, 2).

5 Models for Living

Week 5: Day 1	United in love

Reading: *Philippians 3:17–20*

My brothers, be united in following my rule of life. Take as your models everybody who is already doing this and study them as you used to study us. I have told you often, and I repeat it today with tears, there are many who are behaving as the enemies of the cross of Christ. They are destined to be lost. They make foods into their god and they are proudest of something they ought to think shameful; the things they think important are earthly things. For us, our homeland is in heaven, and from heaven comes the saviour we are waiting for, the Lord Jesus Christ.

We have been reflecting on the fact that Jesus saves us in the context of our life on earth, that our use of the material world is part of our response to his call, and that our attitude towards the world in which we live—its people, its plants, its animals, its mineral resources, its water, its air—reflects our attitude towards God.

We have tried to face honestly some fundamental things in our lives which separate us from God so that through repentance we can return to the path which leads to life and to Jesus. We have gathered together some basic approaches to life which will enable us to recognize Jesus and invite him into our lives, particularly prayerfulness in all aspects of our life, freedom from attachments (material and spiritual), and simplicity, beginning with ourselves and our own situation in life. Today's reading underlines the fact that we are also united with others in our journey through life.

This unity goes beyond the boundaries of time. We travel together and can help and learn from each other. History contains many men and women whose lives show us how and where Jesus is to be found. This week we will consider some of these, but first we must remind ourselves again that our purpose is not first and foremost to save creation from destruction but to serve God. Today's reading points out that the most important things are heavenly things and that the miracle of creation is not our real home. It is our passage home. Our destination is heaven, and it is to bring us there to himself that Jesus came to earth as a baby, walked the earth, and will come again in glory.

The coming of Jesus gives us the first and most important model of the love and motivation we need to carry out the will of God in the world. And it is only through him that we are given the strength and ability to love and serve God in the way he wishes. We can force ourselves with tremendous will-power to undertake rigorous spiritual exercises, meditations through which we subdue our ego and our desires; we can live spartan, ascetic lives in which we shed all dependence on the material world but for the barest minimum of bread and water and a rag to cover us, we can spend everything we have on the poor and devote our lives to caring for them. But for this to become a transforming activity we need Jesus in the midst of what we are doing, making each act an act of love.

Such tremendous feats are possible without his love in our hearts. We can love the idea of being holy, ascetic, generous, living in perfect harmony with our environment—all admirable aims in themselves—but then our motivating force is our own self-satisfaction, self-love. If our eyes are on the heavenly kingdom, our hearts filled with the love of Jesus, then we are not concerned with what we do or the impression we convey. If our only desire is to love God and do his will, then we leave to him the way he asks us to show it. Our only concern is to live in the way we believe God wants, out of love for him, knowing that in this obedience we will encounter Jesus.

My dear people, let us love one another since love comes from God and everyone who loves is begotten by God and knows God.
(1 John 4:7)

Prayer
Glory be to him whose power, working in us, can do infinitely more than

90

we can ask or imagine: glory be to him from generation to generation in
the Church and in Christ Jesus for ever.
(Ephesians 3:20, 21)

Action

Before each task today, try and visualize the person for whom you are
doing it and ask God to help you love them more.

Week 5: Day 2	The cloud of witnesses

Reading: *Hebrews 12:1, 2*

**With so many witnesses in a great cloud on every side of us, we
too, then, should throw off everything that hinders us, especially
the sin that clings so easily, and keep running steadily in the race
we have started. Let us not lose sight of Jesus, who leads us in our
faith and brings it to perfection: for the sake of the joy which was
still in the future, he endured the cross, disregarding the
shamefulness of it, and from now on has taken his place at the
right of God's throne.**

If you are still following these daily reflections then you have started in the race
and will be aware of the great cloud of witnesses who have inspired us in the
past and who are around us now. To run steadily we must unite ourselves with
them and their efforts.

As Christians we have to face the fact that many of those who are at the
forefront of caring for God's creation do not share our beliefs. Some may
even blame the Christian churches for encouraging the destruction of the
earth. Misguided missionary zeal has brought westernization rather than the
love of God to communities whose civilization has subsequently been
destroyed. An exclusive focus on the salvation of souls has left creation
out of the concern of Christians. These are things we have to acknowledge
with humility. They have been failures, not of Christianity, but of our
blindness to the fullness of our faith.

In Isaiah God tells us that 'as the rain and the snow come down from the
heavens and do not return without watering the earth, making it yield and
giving growth to provide seed for the sower and bread for the eating, so the

word that goes from my mouth does not return to me empty, without carrying out my will and succeeding in what it was sent to do' (Isaiah 55:10, 11). We should, therefore, not be surprised if God is using others to fulfil his word and restore understanding of the preciousness of his creation and gifts to humankind. We can now listen to them and welcome their understanding to help us gain a new knowledge of the greatness of our God.

Our strength and commitment lie in the knowledge that it is Jesus who 'leads us in our faith'. We know too that, despite the imperfections of the past, with Jesus to guide us it will at last be brought 'to perfection', and with this perfection will come great joy. We fight side by side with all whose hearts are touched by the plight of creation, for it is God—acknowledged or not, by whatever name he is called—who has touched them.

The time has come to include all creation in our preaching of the good news, and so heed the words of Jesus as he left his disciples: 'Go out to the whole world; proclaim the Good News to all creation.' It is our final chance to show that our faith is real, that it is not merely words. St James writes: 'Take the case, my brothers, of someone who has never done a single good act but claims that he has faith. Will that faith save him? If one of the brothers or one of the sisters is in need of clothes and has not enough food to live on, and one of you says to them, "I wish you well; keep yourself warm and eat plenty", without giving them these bare necessities of life, then what good is that? Faith is like that: if good works do not go with it, it is quite dead ... You believe in the one God—that is creditable enough, but the demons have the same belief, and they tremble with fear' (James 2:14–17, 19).

If, as St Paul says, all 'creation still retains the hope of being freed' (Romans 8:20, 21) and Jesus tells us to preach to all creation, then the importance of St James' message becomes even clearer. Animals, plants, and our natural resources have no need for our words; they need our love, demonstrated daily by our actions.

Prayer
Lord, may we love all your creation, all the earth and every grain of sand in it. May we love every leaf, every ray of your light. May we love the animals: you have given them the rudiments of thought and joy untroubled. Let us not trouble them; let us not harass them, let us not deprive them of their happiness, let us not work against your intent. For we acknowledge unto you that all is like an ocean, all is flowing and blending, and that to withhold any measure of love from anything in your universe is to withhold that same measure from you.

(**Feodor Dostoevsky**, **adapted from** *The Brothers Karamazov*)

Action

Remember in your prayers today all those who work in some way to preserve God's creation.

Week 5: Day 3	**God's wisdom**

Reading: *Romans 11:33–36*

How rich are the depths of God—how deep his wisdom and knowledge—and how impossible to penetrate his motives or understand his methods! Who could ever know the mind of the Lord? Who could ever be his counsellor? Who could ever give him anything or lend him anything? All that exists comes from him; all is by him and for him. To him be the glory for ever! Amen.

Yesterday we reflected on Jesus, who leads us in our faith, as our only hope. Today's reading invites us to reflect again that God's ways are not our ways. It makes me think of the three wise men who came to worship Jesus after his birth. They knew that they were seeking the Messiah, the great king so long anticipated. They might have uttered these words as they entered the stable and found themselves in the presence of poverty and simplicity instead of the royal surroundings they had expected.

St Matthew tells us that the wise men came from a long way off. Their journey was far more arduous than that of the shepherds who were already nearby. No doubt their progress was made even slower by the amount of luggage they had to take with them. The shepherds in their simplicity were told directly where to find the baby and hurried away to find him. The wise men, in their wisdom, had a much harder time of it. Why, one wonders, did they lose sight of the star that had guided them so far? Did they lose sight or lose faith in it when they saw the palace of Herod? They had to learn to abandon their trust in worldly knowledge and set their sights on God alone. By consulting Herod rather than awaiting the next move of the star they set in jeopardy the whole purpose of their journey. Herod, of course, wanted to destroy the child who threatened his supremacy.

There are many warnings in the Old and New Testaments about putting our trust in worldly wisdom. Isaiah tells us that our lack of sincerity in our worship leads us astray in our imagined wisdom. 'Because this people approaches me only in words, honours me only with lip-service, while its heart is far from

93

me . . . The wisdom of its sages shall decay, the intelligence of its intelligent men shall be shrouded' (Isaiah 29:13, 14). St Paul warns us, 'You must live your whole life according to the Christ you have received—Jesus the Lord; you must be rooted in him and built on him and held firm by the faith you have been taught, and full of thanksgiving. Make sure that no one traps you and deprives you of your freedom by some secondhand, empty, rational philosophy based on the principles of this world instead of on Christ' (Colossians 2:6–8).

The wise men were sensible, co-operative people, clever scientists who went to a lot of trouble to find Jesus. Yet, had God not intervened by warning them in a dream not to return to Herod, they might have been instrumental in the destruction of God's plan. We know that it is not possible to destroy God's plan, but we can also see that a failure to trust God and a turning instead to rely on the wisdom of men can have dreadful consequences: hundreds of innocent children had to die. Our cleverness may blind us to God's truth. When the principles of this world are to raise our standards of living, accumulate wealth and property, spend money on space probes and armaments, and all our wise men, our thinkers, are trying to find ways of achieving these aims faster and more successfully, then the language of Jesus, the language of the cross, 'may be illogical to those who are not on the way to salvation, but those of us who are on the way see it as God's power to save' (1 Corinthians 1:18).

Today the language of the cross is as illogical as ever. It tells us, as it always has done, to live more simply, to share rather than to accumulate, to nurture and cherish rather than to own, to live in peace and harmony even if we have to suffer for it, and at all times to acknowledge that 'All that exists comes from him; all is by him and for him. To him be the glory for ever! Amen.'

Prayer

How great and wonderful are all your works, Lord God Almighty; just and true are all your ways, King of nations. Who would not revere and praise your name, O Lord? You alone are holy, and all the pagans will come and adore you for the many acts of justice you have shown.
(Revelation 15:3, 4)

Action

Go through the suggestions for action in this book. Do something you didn't get round to doing. Choose something that you can make into a daily habit.

Reading: *Isaiah 9:1, 2, 5*

The people that walked in darkness has seen a great light; on those who live in a land of deep shadow a light has shone. You have made their gladness greater, you have made their joy increase; they rejoice in your presence as men rejoice at harvest time, as men are happy when they are dividing the spoils . . .

For there is a child born for us, a son given to us and dominion is laid on his shoulders; and this is the name they give him: Wonder-Counsellor, Mighty-God, Eternal-Father, Prince-of-Peace.

The darkness lifts. The deep shadow that lies over us, the difficulties and dangers we face, is pierced by the sun. With Jesus a light shines out and dispels our fears and replaces them with joy and hope.

Look at the four names Isaiah gives the child. Each one gives its own reason for our joy and thanksgiving. Wonder-Counsellor— here at last is the source of the answers to all our questions, the solutions to all our problems. This counsellor is not merely wise; he gives counsel that fills us with wonder, beyond our wildest imaginings. We can bring to him all our deepest terrors and he will soothe us and show us the way to overcome them. He has dominion over all that is. He knows the secrets of the earth and of the heavens. He will illuminate our understanding and show us the path back out of the valley of darkness.

More than that, he is also called Mighty-God. Mighty to do all that he says, to break for all mankind 'the yoke that was weighing on him, the bar across his shoulders, the rod of his oppressor' (verse 3). He has the power to carry out his wonderful counsel, for as we discover in the miracle of his birth, 'Nothing is impossible with God.'

Lest the awe we feel at the wisdom and power of this child before us should keep us away, a third extraordinary name is added: Eternal-Father. We are invited into a relationship of great intimacy and love. A person whose wisdom and power are focused on the good of all his children, who cares for and protects us, who feeds us, picks us up when we stumble, setting us back on our feet, and who leads us to maturity with love and understanding, so that we can be with him eternally in a peace that has no end. For lastly, the child is the Prince-of-Peace, a prince whose rule is based on justice and integrity, whose peace extends into all creation so that:

The wolf lives with the lamb, the panther lies down with the kid, calf and lion cub feed together with a little boy to lead them. The cow and the bear make friends, their young lie down together. The lion eats straw like the ox. The infant plays over the cobra's hole; into the viper's lair the young child puts his hand. They do no hurt, no harm, on all my holy mountain, for the country is filled with the knowledge of Yahweh as the waters swell the sea.

(Isaiah 11:6–9)

This is not poetic imagery. It is a vision of the world where love reigns. The coming of Jesus makes this vision come closer. Let us today ask God to give us a faith that is strong enough to believe in his name, for all these names are one: Wonder-Counsellor, Mighty-God, Eternal-Father, Prince-of-Peace.

Prayer

My Jesus, I worship you. Holy is your Name.

Refer to your balance sheet. Pray about it, asking counsel from the Wonder-Counsellor, power to change from the Mighty-God, loving guidance from the Eternal-Father and peace of mind from the Prince-of-Peace.

Week 5: Day 5   **Sacrifice: St Stephen**

Reading: *Matthew 10:38–39*

'Anyone who does not take up his cross and follow in my footsteps is not worthy of me. Anyone who finds his life will lose it; anyone who loses his life for my sake will find it.'

It is one of the great mysteries of our faith that Jesus, the Son of God, who has all the power that we reflected on yesterday, chose not to use power but sacrifice to accomplish his mission. His complete identification with the suffering of humanity enabled him to give everything, including his life, in order to give us life.

These reflections have been concerned with the suffering of the world in which we live. While we remain observers, sheltered, warm and well fed, the people dying in poverty and degradation are martyrs to our self-love and desire for economic gain. If we can learn to enter into their suffering and begin to identify with the pain of empty stomachs, the cold of homelessness, the anxiety of the unemployed, then gradually we will be able to overcome the pull of our own desires. Through such identification we will be given the strength to deny ourselves and share what we have out of love.

The crisis of the environment and the crisis of poverty has become one. Only if we simplify our own needs to share the resources of the world with others will we also be able to care for the environment. The fate of the earth and its people is the same. As we begin to look at what we have and what we could do without so that others may live, we will see how much we have that is superfluous to our real needs. If we reflect on the mountains of rubbish we generate each week we will see that this too is a sign of the martyrs of our false religion, whose greatest festival is the feast of conspicuous consumption which we celebrate on December 25th. The broken and dying trees and plants, the hunted animals whose habitat is destroyed, the polluted air and water and the general debris of life today, all this is part of the sacrifice.

Jesus tells us that with him we can take upon ourselves the suffering that we see around us. We can take up the cross that will give life to others. Some have done this in a very courageous and direct way, such as the Greenpeace volunteers who risk their lives in non-violent demonstrations to alert the public to the destruction of the living world. In 1985 one of their volunteers became their first 'martyr' when the *Rainbow Warrior* was blown up by the French because of Greenpeace's opposition to the French nuclear testing programme in the Pacific ocean. Their volunteers have faced Soviet whalers, and Canadians culling seals with cudgels; they have demonstrated the effects of chemical effluents on plant and animal life by bathing in polluted rivers, and they have exposed themselves to the risks of cancer in their efforts to bring to our attention the poisoning of the Irish Sea and the local beaches caused by radioactive leads coming from the Sellafield nuclear processing plant. All their protests and all their action is non-violent. But the risks they take provoke violence from others whose interests are threatened by such care for life on earth. For some the violent reactions are very reminiscent of the murderous rage that the members of the Sanhedrin felt when Stephen confronted them with unpalatable truths about their lives in Acts chapter 8.

Few of us feel called to these particular ways of taking up our cross and being prepared to lay down our lives. Most of us can only support the actions of others by joining their organizations, by giving them time and money. But we can all help them in their efforts by becoming more aware of the forces they are confronting, and by examining our own lives to see where we might be inadvertently supporting the destructive processes around us. By reducing our needs and wants we can make a considerable impact on the economic arguments for destroying our environment and causing unnecessary suffering to living creatures and to people.

For those who doubt that Christian martyrdom includes activities other than preaching the gospel or professing belief in Christ, St Stephen, the first Christian martyr, gives some food for thought. He was selected by the church to do a particular job because he was 'a man full of faith and of the Holy Spirit' (Acts 6:5). This job was the daily distribution of food to the poor. In carrying out this humble task he was 'filled with grace and power and began to work miracles and great signs among the people' (Acts 6:8). His enemies hated him for his actions; his words explaining his belief and pointing out their blindness were the final straw.

Prayer

Raise me up when I am most afraid, I put my trust in you; in God, whose word I praise, in God I put my trust, fearing nothing;. what can men do to me?

(Psalm 56:3, 4, 11)

Action

Have a day of 'fasting' once a week by doing without something you take for granted each day, e.g. a newspaper, chocolate bar, drink. Send the fruit of your sacrifice to alleviate poverty.

Week 5: Day 6	The holy family

Reading	*John 13:34, 35*

'I give you a new commandment: love one another; just as I have loved you, you also must love one another. By this love you have for one another, everyone will know that you are my disciples.

The non-violent, caring, sustainable approach to the resources of the world is sometimes called the 'soft' or 'feminine' approach. So-called masculine attributes are blamed for many of today's problems caused by violence, domination and aggression. This analysis has caused inner turmoil to many women, especially Christian women, who find their beliefs expressed in what appears to be male language, with a male God, and whose frustrations seem often to find expression only through aggression and anger at centuries of apparent oppression and disregard for their status. The old order seems to proclaim a 'masculine' Christianity; today many want a 'feminine' faith.

Our task as Christians is, and has always been, to make Jesus present in everything we do and in every encounter we have with each other. Our preoccupation with our own status in this task distracts us from its central purpose, which is to bring Jesus into the world, conceived and brought forth in love. The love 'you have for one another' shows our fidelity to this task.

The first model we have for this task is the Holy Family. This rather shadowy unity in the gospels is the background against which the light of Jesus is first shown to the world. The information we find in the gospels is sometimes conflicting. Matthew gives us the story from the male point of view. Joseph receives the visitation from the angel, is told of the conception of Jesus and is given instructions about the baby's name. Luke, on the other hand, hardly mentions Joseph, except the important point that he 'was of David's House and line' (Luke 1:27; 2:4). He is interested in Mary's part in the story. She is the chosen instrument to bring Christ into the world, to make him visibly present among men.

On their own these two different perspectives would give an unbalanced picture. They would lead us to the mistaken idea that one was more important than the other in bringing Jesus to the world. We would be led into focusing our attention on either Mary or Joseph, away from the whole point of their lives, which was Jesus. Together the evangelists give us the balance that must be in the relationship between the male and the female, the masculine and the feminine, while at the same time emphasizing their unique and different roles. 'Though woman cannot do without man, neither can man do without woman, in the Lord; woman may come from man, but man is born of woman—both come from God' (1 Corinthians 11:11, 12).

Within the Holy Family this harmony and balance between the man and the woman make it possible for the plan of God to be realized and his Son to take human form. It is a harmony that must be reflected in our approach to all the world. Adam and Eve, as one flesh, were both called to care for God's creation. The conflict between them, the domination instead of partnership between man and woman, between them both and the natural world, was brought about by sin. 'To the woman he said, "Your yearning shall be for your husband, yet he will lord it over you"; To the man he said, "Accursed be the soil because of you. With suffering shall you get your food from it every day of your life" ' (Genesis 3:16, 17).

Sin has been overcome by love and sacrifice. Restored harmony between man and woman, husband and wife, is part of a healing process that reaches out beyond mankind into man's relationship with the created world. Love and sacrifice begin within the family. It is the first place in which we encounter God and form our image of him. A mother looking down at her child shows her child the face of God—the child may see a God of love or a God of anger, a caring God, a bullying God, an impatient God, a gentle God. A father caring for his family shows the meaning of the fatherhood of God, the approachable God or the distant, absent God, the dominating God or the gently-leading God. Within the family too is formed our attitude towards the world, an attitude which marks us as Christians and shows the world the God in whom we believe, a God who, today's reading clearly tells us, is only recognizable by love.

Whatever our situation, whether in a family or as single people, the Holy Family teaches us that the love that it radiates to the world is to be based on mutual respect and the bringing together of two distinct and separate elements in order to give birth to the Son of God. The world needs mothering *and* fathering, it needs love based on respect, it needs Jesus to be born in its midst at every moment of every day.

Prayer
Lord God, you are our father and our mother. You have formed us out of the dust of the earth. Help us to love and honour the earth as we do you.

Action
Discuss with your family, or those with whom you live, how you could support each other in developing a lifestyle that is more concerned for others: e.g. all helping with the washing up to avoid using a dishwasher, planning car journeys together to avoid wasteful use of the car, inviting a lonely neighbour to join in special family celebrations.

Week 5: Day 7	Mary

Reading: *Matthew 5:3–12*

'How happy are the poor in spirit; theirs is the kingdom of heaven. Happy the gentle: they shall have the earth for their heritage. Happy those who mourn: they shall be comforted. Happy those who hunger and thirst for what is right: they shall be satisfied. Happy the merciful: they shall have mercy shown them. Happy the pure in heart: they shall see God. Happy the peacemakers: they shall be called sons of God. Happy those who are persecuted in the cause of right: theirs is the kingdom of heaven.

Happy are you when people abuse you and persecute you and speak all kinds of calumny against you on my account. Rejoice and be glad, for your reward will be great in heaven; this is how they persecuted the prophets before you.'

Anyone interested in the lives of great people and their ideas is particularly interested in the influences that shaped those people and the sources of their ideas. Jesus is no exception to such an investigation. Where did his way of thinking come from? In the Beatitudes he seems to turn accepted ways of thinking upside down, fulfilling the words: 'I shall destroy the wisdom of the wise and bring to nothing the learning of the learned.' Who planted the seeds of this understanding which enabled Jesus the man to speak with the voice of God?

If we turn again to the beginning of St Luke and read there the story of the annunciation and Mary's response to the angel, and then her beautiful words to her cousin Elizabeth, it is no longer a mystery why God chose this humble young girl to be the mother of his Son. Her profound insight into the ways of God was the seed-bed in which the divine knowledge that Jesus would have could grow and flourish.

Mary's words in the Magnificat find many echoes in the Beatitudes. The 'exalting' of the 'lowly', the mercy of God 'for those who fear him', the filling of the hungry. Perhaps Jesus had heard such words from her as a child.

More powerful than words, however, was surely Mary's person. Her complete submission to God, 'Let what you have said be done to me'; her suffering for the sake of her son, but holding back for his sake; 'storing up all these things in her heart'; the devotion which eventually enabled her to stand at the foot of the cross and let go even the son God had given her—all these things added up to a life which influenced and shaped Jesus. Then, when confronted with the temptations in the wilderness, he was able to reject any idea of a worldly, powerful Messiah and accept the suffering of the saving Messiah.

The silent, unobtrusive presence of Mary is a challenge to the spirit of our age which we need great courage to embrace. She seems to embody exactly the opposite of that for which most people strive. She did not demand rights, recognition of her own self-fulfilment, and yet she had the self-confidence to speak the words of the Magnificat. 'From this day forward all generations will call me blessed.' Why? Not because of what she had done but because 'The Almighty has done great things for me. Holy is his Name.' Even at this moment of realization—that she was to be the instrument through which God's promise to her ancestors was to be fulfilled—she remained filled with humility, her attention on God, and with concern and joy at his fulfilment of his promises to restore justice to the poor and hungry.

Mary is another model for us to study if we are serious about living out God's will in our lives on his earth. We have to approach our tasks with the same self-less humility. There is no room for ego-building in the work we have to do to save the world's resources, to preserve the beauty and delicacy of the balance of nature about us, to build peace among nations, to feed the hungry. We play our parts as individuals, in families, in local, national and international groups and organizations, because of our love and gratitude to God for his goodness to us, because of our love and gratitude towards the world around us and the good things we are given within it, and out of love and gratitude to the poor, the destitute, the hungry, and sick, the dying, for allowing us to serve our Lord and see him in them.

Prayer
Lord Jesus, I must decrease, you must increase.

Action
Make a list of all the great things God has done for you. Thank him for them and keep the list handy so that you can add to it. Refer to it every time you feel depressed and cast down by your life.

Week 5: **Group discussion and worship—Models for living**

Note for group leader: The aim of this discussion is to become aware that we all have models for living and to ask if they conform to Christian values.

Useful props
1. Pencils and paper.
2. Bible open at Matthew 7:7–11.

Questions for discussion
1. What qualities do you most admire in others? What do you least admire?
2. What figures from history and/or the present day impress you? Why?
3. Who most embodies Christian teaching for you?

4. What are you most proud of in your life and achievements? Why?
5. Which of the qualities, positive and negative, raised in (1) apply to Jesus?
6. Do you think that your church encourages you to foster those attributes you most value in its worship/social activities/pastoral care?

Preparation for worship
1. Prepare a prayer of thanksgiving for the person or people who most inspire and encourage you to live like Christ.
2. Each choose one Christ-like quality that they would like to receive and that the rest of the group agree with.

Suggestions for worship

◇ **Read Psalm 1.**

◇ **Each pray their prayer of thanksgiving.**

◇ **Read Matthew 7:7–11.**

◇ **Each says, 'We ask you, Lord, for …' and lays their 'quality' by the open Bible.**

◇ **Leader prays: 'We pray continually that our God will make you worthy of his call, and by his power fulfil all your desires for goodness and complete all that you have been doing through faith; because in this way the name of our Lord Jesus Christ will be glorified in you and you in him, by the grace of our God and the Lord Jesus Christ' (2 Thessalonians 1:11, 12).**

6 *Celebrating Creation*

Reading: *Luke 19:35–40*

So they took the colt to Jesus, and throwing their garments over its back they helped Jesus on to it. As he moved off, people spread their cloaks in the road, and now, as he was approaching the downward slope of the Mount of Olives, the whole group of disciples joyfully began to praise God at the top of their voices for all the miracles they had seen. They cried out:
'Blessings on the King who comes, in the name of the Lord! Peace in heaven and glory in the highest heavens.'
Some Pharisees in the crowd said to him, 'Master, check your disciples,' but he answered, 'I tell you, if these keep silence the stones will cry out.'

The story of Jesus's triumphant entry into Jerusalem is so important that all four gospels record it. At last Jesus allows the people to celebrate his kingship by their homage and rejoicing. They give no thought for themselves in their desire to acclaim him as king. Their clothes are sacrificed, to be trampled on by the donkey and, no doubt, by the crowd that followed. Branches and greenery were thrown in front of the donkey too for good measure, according to the other three evangelists.

The disciples were overcome with joy 'praising God at the top of their voices for all the miracles they had seen.' Jesus was being recognized for who he was at last and the words with which they praise God expressed their joy that the Messiah had come to claim his own and fulfil the promise of God to send a Saviour and King to his people. Heaven itself was rejoicing at this great moment. Everyone was jubilant except for the Pharisees who, as usual, were affronted and shocked that Jesus should allow such praise.

Jesus's answer is in itself a new prophecy that is being fulfilled today. He says that if he is not praised and acknowledged as King then the stones will cry out and the stones are indeed crying out today for our lack of acknowledgement that Jesus Christ is King of all creation. Not merely the stones, but the trees, the water and all creation. They are asking us to praise and reverence the Lord for all the miracles we see about us today. They are crying out to us to throw down all that we have before him so that he can ride triumphantly into our lives and hearts.

Every day we witness miracles around us: the birth of a child, the blossoming of trees in spring, the sweetness of honey from the labour of the bee, the beauty of a spider's web bejewelled by autumn dew. Jesus said that 'anyone who does not welcome the kingdom of God like a little child will never enter it' (Mark 10:15). Little children welcome the kingdom of God because their eyes are open to the wonder about them as they watch an ant scurrying past with its huge burden in its mouth and notice the pink tinge around the petals of a daisy. The joy and wonder in their eyes is true praise.

Those who can see the world around them with awe and wonder are experiencing the presence of God in their lives. As Jesus drew near to Jerusalem he was filled with sorrow. He said, 'If you in your turn had only understood this day the message of peace! But, alas, it is hidden from your eyes!' Let us today open our eyes and join with creation in singing and living the praise of God our Creator and Jesus our King.

Prayer

Acclaim Yahweh, all the earth, burst into shouts of joy! Sing to Yahweh, sing to the music of harps, and to the sound of many instruments; Let the sea thunder and all that it holds, and the world with all who live in it; let all the rivers clap their hands and the mountains shout for joy.
(Psalm 98 [97]:4–8)

Action

Make Sundays the day of the Lord of creation. Try to avoid celebrating the

Lord's day in ways that harm his creation (like unnecessary driving). Walk or cycle to your nearest park, if you have no garden of your own, and spend some time looking carefully at the beauty of living things. Join them in praise.

Week 6: Day 2   Joy—St Francis of Assisi

Reading: *Psalm 150:1–6*

Praise God in his holy place, praise him in his mighty heavens, praise him for his powerful deeds, praise him for his surpassing greatness.
O praise him with sound of trumpet, praise him with lute and harp, praise him with timbrel and dance, praise him with strings and pipes.
O praise him with resounding cymbals, praise him with clashing of cymbals. Let everything that lives and breathes give praise to the Lord.
The Psalms: a new translation © **1963 The Grail, Collins Fontana**

This psalm makes me think of St Francis of Assisi—that saint we all love, who called himself and his friars 'God's jugglers'. He is the patron saint of all who care about God's creation. His life is a feast of love for everything that God creates. With the example of St Francis before us we should turn back again to the first chapter of Genesis and re-read the story of creation. After each day, when we read 'and God saw that it was good', we should then add, 'and therefore I will love, cherish and reverence it. Thanks be to God.'

The mark of the Christian is joy, and this joy is not dimmed by the seriousness of the task we have before us. We are not merely echoing the words of prophets of doom; we will 'gird our loins' and act out of hope for the future.

St Paul advises us to look for 'models' to study. St Francis is one of these 'models'. His joy grew out of his love and his simplicity. While the Franciscans' way of life, in its extreme form of poverty and lack of any possessions, is not one that most of us are able to embrace, we can still learn a great deal from their complete trust in God to provide all their needs and the consequent love and reverence for nature as the source of the gifts of life.

The simplicity which St Francis practised is that simplicity which Jesus lived. We have not always been faithful to it in our Christian history and reformers have had to bring the message back to us time and again. Luther, John Fox and John Wesley are just a few examples. Today new reformers are calling for simplicity. Like St Francis, their simplicity and their love of nature are linked. They are our new models—hundreds of individuals putting the care of the earth and its resources before their own wants and satisfactions, but finding that their acts of generosity and of sacrifice give them joy and greater love.

We must seek out such people to inspire us. An elderly retired man in Gloucestershire plants tree seedlings in his little plot of land. When they are big enough to transplant he gives them to the local council to plant on roadsides and parks, around schools and housing estates. (Even a flat dweller could collect acorns and horse chestnuts and plant them in flowerpots to transplant them when they are large enough into a suitable piece of public land.) In West London a group of people, by hard work and persistence, persuaded London Transport to let them turn a derelict patch of land between train tracks into a nature reserve. Such group efforts are taking place all over the country. Every individual can increase his or her effectiveness by joining a group.

On our own we can make an impact too. Sufficient numbers of individuals now use recycled paper for writing and printing (as well as for toilet paper and tissue) that it has become possible to produce it competitively both in terms of price and quality.

The extraordinary diversity of our vegetable and fruit varieties is being kept alive by many individuals who grow them in gardens and allotments. Such seeds are no longer commercially available and can only be obtained by joining the Henry Doubleday Association, which is devoted to saving plant diversity for future generations. Why should we bother? Because disease or pest could wipe out an entire food variety if the plant species is lost. (Today 95% of our food comes from only 30 species of food crop.)

All these acts are in the spirit of St Francis and those who carry them out are the true Friends of the Earth as he was. Through them 'everything that lives and breathes', so abused by the greed of mankind, is able, once more, to 'give praise to the Lord'.

Prayer

Praise be my Lord for our mother the earth, the which doth sustain us and keep us, and bringeth forth divers fruits and flowers of many colours, and grass.

Praise ye and bless the Lord and give thanks unto him and serve him with great humility.

(St Francis)

Action

Discuss with your church leadership ways in which you could share your concern and love for God's creation with your church.

Week 6: Day 3   **Love spans many generations**

Reading: *Psalm 103:13–18*

As tenderly as a father treats his children, so Yahweh treats those who fear him; he knows what we are made of, he remembers we are dust.
Man lasts no longer than grass, no longer than a wild flower he lives, one gust of wind, and he is gone, never to be seen there again; yet Yahweh's love for those who fear him lasts from all eternity and for ever, like his goodness to their children's children, as long as they keep his covenant and remember to obey his precepts.

The Psalmist was acutely aware of the incomprehensibility of God's love. Today we read again of this mystery. God, from his perspective of eternity, knows that the life of man is insignificant—'one gust of wind and he is gone'—yet he loves each one as tenderly as a father loves his children. In fact he loves even more than that for his love lasts 'all eternity and for ever'. This extraordinary love goes beyond that of a father for his children; it extends to their children's children. It is a love that goes from generation to generation.

The Bible, assuming the constancy and depth of parental love, often makes use of it as a pointer to the love of God which is so much greater. 'Does a woman forget her baby at the breast, or fail to cherish the son of her womb? Yet even if these forget, I will never forget you' (Isaiah 49:15); Jesus himself says, 'If you, then, who are evil, know how to give your children what is good, how much more will your Father in heaven give good things to those who ask him!' (Matthew 7:11).

I wonder whether the same images would have been used if these passages had been written today. We no longer take for granted the deep enduring bond between parent and child. Countless women have abandoned the 'son of their womb' by abortion, assuming it to be their right. Many more treat children as another possession competing with a new fridge, video, new car or larger house. It is only the rich who seem not to be able to afford to have children. And all of us,

108

by the way we live, are trading off our children's future against our present wants. As we destroy the world around us to satisfy our demands, we leave a bleak prospect for future generations, while at the same time we are teaching them, by our example, to believe that the only kind of life worth living is one in which every whim and desire is immediately fulfilled. By our greed today we leave our children in need tomorrow. Today's victims are the people of the Third World; tomorrow's are our children.

Today's reading puts a very different kind of love before us. It is a love which goes beyond self and beyond time, which embraces all that is to come. Perhaps our different concept and practice of parental love, and of care of one generation for the next, prevents us from understanding the love God has for us. It is easier to understand that 'man lasts no longer than grass, no longer than a wild flower he lives'. Short-term views mean much more than long-term ones. But the present world crisis challenges us to come to terms with the long-term—even eternal—nature of love and in so doing reflect God more perfectly.

Let us begin afresh to live in a way in which our care for our children's future takes priority over our own desires. Let our care for the world we have to pass on to them be the sign of our love for them. Let us recognize that anything we do that encourages them to treat the earth as something there solely for the purpose of satisfying their desires is giving them stones not bread. Let us reflect on the image of today's reading which reminds us that God's love for us is for all time, even though we are as passing in the world as are the plants and the grass. It is an image that reminds us that we too must regard nature with the same enduring love; the grass which is here today and dies tomorrow must be cared for so that it can appear again the day after. Our care for the living, natural world shows that our love for our children is also 'for eternity and for ever'.

In doing this we will not only be loving them with real love by ensuring that they have a future, but we will be giving them the opportunity to glimpse the meaning and depth of the love of God.

Prayer

Lord God, may our care for the world and its resources be inspired by that same love which you have for us, a love which reaches out from you, through us, to our children's children.

Action

Share your love of one aspect of creation with a child today by pointing out something beautiful—real or in a picture.

Reading: *1 John 2:7–10*

My dear people, this is not a new commandment that I am writing to tell you, but an old commandment that you were given from the beginning, the original commandment which was the message brought to you. Yet in another way, what I am writing to you, and what is being carried out in your lives as it was in his, is a new commandment; because the night is over and the real light is already shining. Anyone who claims to be in the light but hates his brother is still in the dark. But anyone who loves his brother is living in the light and need not be afraid of stumbling.

The life of Jesus brought to fulfilment centuries of Jewish belief and waiting for the Messiah. He came to explain the true meaning of the Law and the messages of the prophets and, in his life, not only to demonstrate this meaning but to take upon himself generations of sin and guilt which had separated the chosen people from their God. What he had to say was essentially the same as the prophets had said, yet, at the same time, it was radically new.

Jesus was directing the Jews' attention back to the essentials of their faith and developing that greatest commandment of all, 'You must love the Lord your God with all your heart, with all your soul, and with all your mind. This is the greatest and the first commandment. The second resembles it: You must love your neighbour as yourself. On these two commandments hang the whole Law, and the Prophets also' (Matthew 22:37–40). And St John shows us throughout his writings that these two commandments are inseparable, that our love for God is shown by our love for our neighbour.

What was quite different from the old Jewish attitude towards God was that with Christ it was no longer an exclusive religion but became universal. All men and women, throughout the world, could become children of God, chosen people, saved through Jesus Christ.

Our freedom in Christ from Jewish Law has tended to blind us to the fact that the teachings of Jesus were related to that Law, and that the Evangelists and St Paul were Jews who were thoroughly acquainted with their Jewish heritage. While we understand that the New Testament fulfils the Old, we do not always fully appreciate that the Old Testament leads us to the New Testament and to a fuller understanding of Jesus and our faith.

In October 1982 young Jews and Christians met together to explore the meaning of their faith in the context of today's ecological and environmental crisis. They were addressed by Rabbis and by Christian pastors, but much of their time was spent in joint Bible study. In the six days they were together some of them discovered in their own way that while the truth of 'the original commandments' remains unchanged, the law of love shows a new and vital interpretation for today's problems. They united the old and the new in the form of ten ecological commandments.

1. I am the Lord your God who has created heavens and earth. Know that you are my partner in creation; therefore, take care of the air, water, earth, plants and animals, as if they were your brothers and sisters.

2. Know that in giving you life I have given you responsibility, freedom and limited resources.

3. Steal not from the future; honour your children by giving them a chance at longevity.

4. Implant in your children a love of nature.

5. Remember that humanity can use technology, but cannot recreate life that has been destroyed.

6. Set up pressure groups within your community to prevent impending catastrophes.

7. Throw out all arms which cause irreversible destruction to the foundations of life.

8. Be self-disciplined in the small details of your life.

9. Set aside time in your weekly day of rest to be with the world rather than to use the world.

10. Remember that you are not the owner of the land, merely its guardian.

'My children, our love is not to be just words or mere talk, but something real and active ... Whoever keeps his commandments lives in God and God lives in him' (1 John 3:18, 24).

Prayer
Lord, teach us to understand your commandments in all their depth and to love them as the source of life through your Son.

Action
Reflect on these 'commandments' and choose one to guide all you do today.

111

Reading: *John 12:31–33*

'Now sentence is being passed on this world; now the prince of this world is to be overthrown. And when I am lifted up from the earth, I shall draw all men to myself.' By these words he indicated the kind of death he would die.

In some translations of the Bible the word 'tree' is used instead of the word 'cross' for that upon which Jesus died. For the Jews Jesus' death on a tree had associations of the most extreme rejection, for in the Law was written that those who were hanged on a tree were cursed before God (Deuteronomy 21:22, 23). On the tree Jesus became identified with the lowest of the low (see Galatians 3:13). At the same time they also knew that trees were the source of shelter and special blessing to which sin had prevented them access since Adam and Eve were banished from the Garden of Eden lest they ate from the tree of life.

It is perhaps time to revive the association between the cross and the tree in a very literal sense. Both are central to our lives and our survival on earth and in eternity. Jesus says that his death on the cross will draw all men to himself. He meant that it would unite mankind in their love and response to his sacrifice. This unity still awaits completion. Our witness to Christ has not been adequate to show mankind the attracting qualities of the cross. The tree from which the cross was made is now beginning to speak for itself and bring mankind together in a new understanding of its value.

The suffering borne by Jesus on the cross is reflected now by the suffering of mankind throughout the world where trees have been abused. It is as if their suffering is giving us another chance to unite at the foot of the cross on which Jesus was lifted up over the world, by returning to an ancient, yet new, understanding of the meaning of the tree of life.

Concern about trees is shared world-wide by the people most affected. Many of them are of other religions. In India the Himalayan forests have been regarded as sacred for centuries. The failure of Western timber merchants to respect this was a sign of their failure to understand the ways of God. It was obvious that a violation of this sanctity would lead to devastating floods and droughts. Gandhi used to urge that every Indian should plant one tree a year, for five years. This was based on Buddhist teaching. He believed that this would solve India's problems. Today it is women and children who are waking up to the truths held in these ancient teachings. Schoolchildren in Gujarat, whose family duties include collecting fuel by cutting down scrub and trees, are collecting and planting more seedlings than all the government agencies put together. The children whose future is in jeopardy have taken their future into their own hands. They are putting new meaning into the words of their national poet Rabindranath Tagore who said that a tree is 'the creative power in its peaceful form'. It is a most positive form of non-violent revolution where revolution means changing the face of the country for the good of its people.

Women too are foremost in these forms of non-violent change. Out of the sacred foothills of the Himalayas has come the Chipko Andolan or 'Hug-the-trees' movement, born out of village women's concern about the deforestation that is threatening their existence. Their traditional role of collecting fuel and fodder for their communities has been extended into one which ensures fuel and fodder supplies for their children as well as preserving the land resources which otherwise are destroyed by floods and landslides. Their voluntary reafforestation work is an example to the world and unites them with women elsewhere who have had the same vision to extend their care for their children and their communities into care for their future. Wangari Maathai, one of the leading women in a similar movement in Kenya, says simply, 'Because we are human beings we have the capacity to care.' This care that we have simply because we are humans beings is what unites us at the foot of the cross and can unite us now, whatever our religion, in the cause of all humanity.

Prayer

You died on the cross to free us. Let our concern and care today for the trees of the world be an expression of our gratitude to the tree which held your body above the world to draw all men to yourself in love.

Action

Resolve to be responsible for planting a tree this year. If you do not have a suitable garden then find someone who has. Perhaps a special present for an anniversary, or a leaving present for your child's school?

Week 6: Day 6   **Work for living**

Reading: *1 Corinthians 9:17, 18*

If I had chosen this work myself, I might have been paid for it, but

**as I have not, it is a responsibility which has been put into my
hands. Do you know what my reward is? It is this: in my preaching,
to be able to offer the Good News free, and not insist on the rights
which the gospel gives me.**

'A responsibility put into our hands.' We are a chosen generation. We have been
chosen out of all the millions that have gone before us to decide whether life on
this planet will continue or whether it will die out. We cannot ignore this choice.
If we refuse to take on the responsibility we are deciding against life. We have not
chosen this work. We have been chosen for it. Our reward is the knowledge that
we do God's will and that this is the way we have been called to witness to his
love and truth today.

Yesterday we looked at some examples of people who have taken the
responsibility for the future into their own hands. These people could well sit
back and tell us to do it. Their poverty and the famine they face is closely related
to our prosperity. But they have chosen to take the responsibility back into their
own hands where they can.

Nevertheless, as we have seen over the last few weeks, our responsibility
remains and it is closely tied up with our witness to the truth, to the way we
preach the gospel with our lives rather than our lips. We can join numerous
pressure groups, attend conferences, lobby MPs, and it is important that we do
so, but we must also witness with our lives in a direct manner. The Lifestyle
Movement has as its slogan the Gandhian words: 'Live simply so that others may
simply live.' It is our willingness to do this that puts teeth into our campaigning.

Perhaps the closest we can get to guidelines on how to live simply is the rule
of St Benedict. Although for monks, it is a rule devised with human frailty in
mind. It shows us that living simply does not mean uncomfortable deprivation
but a balanced life in which we avoid accumulation and attachment to things not
essential for a decent life. As St Paul says: 'As long as the readiness is there, a man
is acceptable with whatever he can afford; never mind what is beyond his means.
This does not mean that to give relief to others you ought to make things difficult
for yourselves: it is a question of balancing what happens to be your surplus now
against their present need, and one day they may have something to spare that
will supply your own need' (2 Corinthians 8:12–14).

At the centre of St Benedict's rule is the balance between prayer, work and
learning. Our simplicity is based on the integration of these three activities.
Knowledge is important so that we understand how our lives interact with that
of others, how what we buy might cause suffering to wildlife and nature in
general, or increase the poverty of others. We have to work to overcome these
injustices, and we have to underpin everything we do, every decision we make,
with prayer.

In St Benedict's day work meant manual labour. Today this is an element that is missing from many people's lives. In an effort to simplify our lives it is often helpful to choose one area in which we try to do something for ourselves rather than buy the finished product. Something that is essential and life-giving. Growing vegetables (even in a small way in window boxes!) is one way. To do this by nurturing rather than by using chemicals and fertilizers is a way of coming closer to the ways of God through 'work'. What a miracle compost is! All our waste matter turns back into rich life-giving soil. This exercise teaches us more than any other that a recycling economy is one with a viable future.

My own way is baking bread. I am lucky enough to have a mill to grind my wheat into flour. (Alas, not a garden in which to grow the wheat.) Each week I witness the reality of the parable of the yeast leavening the whole batch of dough. I see the miracle of the simple ingredients of flour, water and yeast transform into the life-sustaining bread which my children devour with as much relish as any cake or biscuit. It shows the whole family the richness of the simple.

There has been a great movement back to the 'simple life', in some cases by a move back into the country to a small-holding and self-sufficiency. It is something we should all think about as Christians, not by moving house but by looking into our lives and finding a new balance in our lifestyle which has as its centre Christ our Lord.

Prayer
Give me neither poverty or riches,
grant me only my share of bread to eat.
(Proverbs 30:8)

Action
Look at your basic needs and choose something that you buy ready-made that you could do for yourself. How about making your own jam or marmalade? Re-using jam jars is much better than recycling, which uses energy. Surprise your friends and fill their empty jam jars. For an extra special Christmas present add a little alcohol to the jam just before bottling!

Reading: *2 Peter 1:3–8*

> By his divine power, he has given us all the things that we need for
> life and for true devotion, bringing us to know God himself, who
> has called us by his own glory and goodness. In making these gifts,
> he has given us the guarantee of something very great and
> wonderful to come: through them you will be able to share the
> divine nature and to escape corruption in a world that is sunk in
> vice. But to attain this, you will have to do your utmost yourselves,
> adding goodness to the faith that you have, understanding to your
> goodness, self-control to your understanding, patience to your
> self-control, true devotion to your patience, kindness towards your
> fellow men to your devotion, and, to this kindness, love. If you have
> a generous supply of these, they will not leave you ineffectual or
> unproductive: they will bring you to a real knowledge of our Lord
> Jesus Christ.

In this passage St Peter gives us our blueprint for survival. His description of the
call to Christian living assumes the unity of creation, the interplay between the
physical and the spiritual. In the same sentence he brings together what 'we
need for life' and what we need 'to know God'. While always reminding us that
our true destiny is heaven, he does not evade our tasks on earth.

We have been given all things we need for life but Peter does not add 'so use
them without restraint and as you wish'. No, he adds 'we will have to do our
utmost' so that through them we 'will be able to share the divine nature and
escape corruption'.

His list of qualities needed to be effective is more like a programme of work.
He does not expect us to be totally transformed instantaneously, but to work
step by step. First we start with faith, the foundation-stone. But it is not enough if
we are to live our lives fully as Christians, because our actions must bear witness
to our faith. We have to add goodness. We also have to use our minds. But our
minds often mislead us, so Peter says 'understanding' rather than thinking. This
implies wisdom, something entering our minds from outside, enlightening us.
Recognizing the dangers that can enter if our minds are let loose without proper
understanding (as E. F. Schumacher often said, 'We are much too clever to be
able to survive without wisdom'), St Peter advises us to add self-control. This
adds the use of the will. So the heart, the mind and the will must all be brought to
bear on living out our Christian vocation in the world.

All this is very hard work and so we need to add patience. This is one of the

116

most difficult virtues to acquire these days. Everything is in a rush, we wish to attain results quickly, *instant* is the watchword of our times. Patience is the watchword of nature—waiting, caring, not grumbling, allowing things to grow. It is essential too in the things of God. He does not give us instant answers, we do not become instant saints, we cannot transform and renew the world instantaneously. We can only begin now.

Once we have begun, we must resist the temptation to be constantly examining our progress. We must leave that to God, otherwise we are like gardeners who, anxious to see whether a plant is growing, pull it up by the roots, and in so doing stunt it, if not kill it. So we need patience, understanding that it takes time and hard work to become more God-like, to become whole—holy. As soon as we become concerned about ourselves we are turning away from God. While we look at God we cannot see ourselves.

We have before us the divine example—the baby in the manger, helpless, bound by the restraints of time. Jesus had to grow, develop and learn before he could accomplish his task. With his help we too will eventually learn to walk with him and so accomplish the tasks he gives us.

Prayer

Give me a pure heart—that I may see thee,
A humble heart—that I may hear thee,
A heart of love—that I may serve thee,
A heart of faith—that I may abide in thee.
(Dag Hammarskjöld, *Markings*)

Action

Pray slowly the prayer of Charles de Foucauld:
Father, I abandon myself into your hands.
Do with me what you will.
Whatever you may do I thank you.
I am ready for all, I accept all,
Let only your will be done in me and in all your creatures.
I wish no more than this, O Lord.
Into your hands I commend my soul,
I offer it to you with all the love of my heart,
For I love you Lord, and so need to give myself,
To surrender myself into your hands
Without reserve and with boundless confidence.
For you are my father.

Note for group leader: The aim of this discussion is to bring together the discussions of the last six weeks and to plan further action together.

Useful props
1. Pencils and paper.
2. Cross decorated with flowers.
3. Symbols to represent what the discussions have meant to each person.

Questions for discussion
1. What have you found useful about these group discussions and worship?
2. How could you widen the discussion into your church community through action or worship?
3. What action could you in your group take in the community? Remember that everything you do however small is of significance. If several of you do it together it is even more significant.
4. How could you, as a group, help each other? e.g. share cars or car journeys, share an allotment, buy in bulk and share contents and so save packaging ...

Preparation for worship
1. Find a symbol to express what you feel about the last six weeks' discussions and Bible study.
2. Prepare a prayer to express this.

Suggestions for worship

◇ **Read Psalm 30 [29].**

◇ **Each pray their prayer and place their symbol in front of the cross.**

◇ **Say together: Jesus said, 'I have come that they may have life and have it to the full.' Lord, give us that life so that we may work together to bring it to all creation.**

◇ **Read Revelation 21:1–5.**

Table 1   Table showing the relationship between population growth and resource consumption

Energy consumption is a very useful indicator of resource consumption in general because it is required for all industrial production as well as modern agricultural production

	population (millions)	commercial energy use (bill. mill. BTUs)	per capita energy use (million BTUs)
USA	232	75.1	324
UK	56	7.7	152
India	717	4.9	7
China	1008	17.9	17

This table illustrates that level of energy consumption is not related to population level but to level of industrialization. While China uses somewhat over double the UK's energy levels commercially, the UK's population is in fact almost one twentieth that of China.

Table 2

In this table it is assumed that US and UK populations and energy consumption remains stable while that of India and China both double. (This effectively means a fourfold increase in commercial energy use by India and China.)

	population (millions)	commercial energy use (as above)	per capita energy use (as above)
USA	232	75.1	324
UK	56	7.7	152
India	1434	19.6	14
China	2016	71.6	34

Note that China with a population now *assumed* to be nearly 9 times that of the USA is approaching the *actual current* rate of US commercial energy use. India's new *assumed* level of consumption is about 2.5 times that of the UK whereas the assumed population increase makes India's population almost 26 times larger than the UK.

Useful Addresses

British Trust for Conservation Volunteers (organize working holidays in UK
 and overseas)
36 St Mary's Street
WALLINGFORD
Oxon OX10 0EU
0491 39766

Campaign Against the Arms Trade
5 Caledonian Road
LONDON N1 9DX
071 281 0297

CAFOD (Catholic Relief Agency)
2 Romero Close
Stockwell Road
LONDON SW9 9TY
071 733 7900

Christian Aid
35–41 Lower Marsh
LONDON SE1 7RL
071 620 4444
Ireland: 0232 381204
Scotland: 031 220 1254
Wales: 0222 614435

Christian CND
11 Goodwin Street
LONDON N4 3HQ
071 700 2393

Christians Aware
10 Springfield Road
LEICESTER LE2 3BD
0533 708831

Christian Ecology Link
20 Carlton Road
HARROGATE
North Yorks HG2 8DD
0423 871616

Forest Friends (recycled paper products)
Badgworth Barns
Notting Hill Way
Weare, AXBRIDGE
Somerset BS26 2JU
0934 732469

Friends of the Earth
377 City Road
LONDON
EC1V 1NA
071 490 1555

Greenpeace
Canonbury Villas
LONDON N1 2PN
071 354 5100

Lifestyle Movement
Manor Farm
LITTLE GIDDING
Huntingdon PE17 5RJ
08323 383

Methodist World Development Programme
1 Central Buildings
Storeys Gate
Westminster
LONDON SW1H 9NH
071 222 8010

Oxfam
274 Banbury Road
OXFORD OX2 7DZ
0865 56777

Pax Christi
9 Henry Street
LONDON N4 2LH
081 800 4612

Quaker Peace Service
Friends House
Euston Road
LONDON NW1 2BJ
071 387 3601

Tear Fund
100 Church Road
TEDDINGTON
Middlesex TW11 8QE
081 977 9144

Traidcraft
Kingsway
GATESHEAD NE11 0NE
091 487 3191

Women's World Day of Prayer
62 London Road
MAIDSTONE
Kent
ME16 8QL
0622 677064

World Wide Fund for Nature
Panda House
Weyside Park
GODALMING
Surrey GU7 1XR
0483 426444

Sources

Biblical quotations are taken from the Jerusalem Bible, published by Darton, Longman & Todd Ltd, and Doubleday & Company Inc. 1966, 1967 and 1968.

Elizabeth Goudge, *St Francis of Assisi*, Duckworth 1959.
Service of the Heart, Union of Liberal and Progressive Synagogues, London 1967/5728.
Donald Nicholl, *Holiness*, Darton, Longman & Todd 1981.
E. F. Schumacher, *Future is Manageable*, Impex, India, 1978
Barry Commoner, *The Closing Circle*, quote in Friends of the Earth Handbook, Heinemann Educational, 1987
Richard Foster, *Freedom of Simplicity*, Triangle 1981.
E. F. Schumacher, *Modern Pressures and the Environment*, November 1972, from the private papers of Mrs V. Schumacher.
The Radical Bible, Spectrum Publications.
E. F. Schumacher, *The Economics of Conservation*, 1970, from the private papers of Mrs V. Schumacher.
John Dalrymple, *Longest Journey*, Darton, Longman & Todd 1979.
Mother Teresa, *A Gift for God*, Fount Paperbacks 1981.
Stefan Wyszynski, *Our Father*, St Paul Paperbacks 1982.
John XXIII, *Journal of a Soul*, Chapman 1980.
Ten Ecological Commandments, 'From the Martin Buber House', International Council of Christians and Jews.
State of the World Reports, World Watch Institute, W. W. Norton & Co (New York), 1985, 1987, 1991
Lloyd Timberlake, *Only One Earth*, BBC Publications 1987.

Material quoted from *Holiness* by Donald Nicholl and from *Longest Journey* by John Dalrymple used by permission of the publishers, Darton, Longman and Todd.

More titles from the Bible Reading Fellowship:

New Daylight
A pattern for daily Bible reading

Edited by Shelagh Brown

Each day's reading contains a Bible passage (printed out in full, from the version chosen by the contributor), along with a brief commentary and explanation, and a suggestion for prayer, meditation or reflection.

The sections of comment often draw on and reflect the experiences of the contributors themselves and thus offer contemporary and personal insights into the readings.

Sunday readings focus on the themes of Prayer and Holy Communion.

New Daylight is published three times a year, in January, May and September.

New Daylight is also available in a large print version.

Individual subscriptions (direct from BRF) covering 3 issues for under 5 copies, payable in advance (including postage & packing) at £7.50 each p.a. (Large print £12.00 each p.a.)

Group subscriptions (direct from BRF) covering 3 issues for 5 copies or more, sent to one address (post free) at £6.00 each p.a. (Large print £10.50 each p.a.)

Copies may also be obtained from Christian bookshops at £2.00 each (Large print £3.50 per copy).

With effect from May 1992 these prices will change to £7.95 each p.a. for individual subscriptions, £6.15 each p.a. for group subscriptions and £2.15 p.a. each for copies from Christian bookshops. Large print prices will not change.

Guidelines to the Bible

*Week by week Bible reading for thought,
prayer and action*

Edited by Grace Emmerson and John Parr

Guidelines contains running commentary, with
introductions and background information, arranged in
weekly units. Each week's material is usually broken up into at
least six sections. Readers can take as much or as little at a time
as they wish. The whole 'week' can be used at a sitting, or split
up into convenient parts: this flexible arrangement allows for
one section to be used each weekday. A Bible will be needed.
The last section of each week is usually called 'Guidelines' and
has points for thought, meditation and prayer. A short list of
books, to help with further reading, appears at the end of some
contributions.

    Guidelines is published three times a year, in
January, May and September.

Individual subscriptions (direct from BRF) covering 3 issues for under 5
copies, payable in advance (including postage & packing) at £7.95 each p.a.

Group subscriptions (direct from BRF) covering 3 issues for 5 copies or more,
sent to one address (post free) at £6.45 each p.a.

Copies may also be obtained from Christian bookshops at £2.15 each.

With effect from May 1992 these prices will change to £7.95 each p.a. for
individual subscriptions, £6.15 each p.a. for group subscriptions and £2.15
p.a. each for copies from Christian bookshops.

First Light
Bible activities for children

Edited by Jan Ainsworth

First Light notes set out to make Bible reading fun—but thoughtful fun.

The notes are designed to bring the Bible alive and involve readers with the help of quizzes, puzzles and activities all based on the *Alternative Service Book* Sunday readings.

First Light can be used at home, church or in Sunday School.

Notes for group leaders are available with each issue, with advice and suggestions on how to use *First Light*.

First Light notes are fully illustrated and are written by a team of contributors—Jan Ainsworth, Diane Webb, Sharon Swain and Judith Sadler.

First Light is published three times a year, in January, May and September.

Individual subscriptions (direct from BRF) covering 3 issues for under 5 copies, payable in advance (including postage & packing) at £7.95 each p.a.

Group subscriptions (direct from BRF) covering 3 issues for 5 copies or more, sent to one address (post free) at £6.45 each p.a.

Copies may also be obtained from Christian bookshops at £2.15 each.

With effect from May 1992 these prices will change to £7.95 each p.a. for individual subscriptions, £6.15 each p.a. for group subscriptions and £2.15 each p.a. for copies from Christian bookshops.